Pharmacognosy & Nutrition

Volume-1

Chief Editor

Neelesh Kumar Maurya

Co-Editor

Radha Kushwaha □ Dr. Hari Shyam

VIRGIN SAHITYAPEETH

Publisher

VIRGIN SAHITYAPEETH
9971275250 / virginsahityapeeth@gmail.com

Copyright

Disclaimer

I hereby declare that this book contains invited chapters and not autonomous work. All sources and aids used have been indicated as such. All texts, either quoted directly or paraphrased have been indicated by in-text citations. Full bibliographic details are given in the reference list which also contains internet sources containing URL and access date. This work has not been submitted to any other examination authority.

Contents

Chapter-1

PHARMACOGNOSY OF FLAVONOIDS IN OBESITY

Goel Bharti

Department of Foods and Nutrition, Government Home Science College, Punjab University, Chandigarh, India

ABSTRACT

In this current scenario, obesity and diabetes are increasing worldwide as obesity is the condition that results in weight gain by increasing excessive body weight which is associated with many factors such as genetic factors, socioeconomic status, sedentary lifestyle and more inclusion of processed foods in the diet. So, there are various ways to prevent obesity and diabetes as physical exercise, healthy diet, and natural constituent as Flavonoids for developing safe products that are present in plants which is responsible for various properties as an antioxidant, anti-diabetes and also to combat obesity as anthocyanins, flavonols, flavones, flavanones, flavans-3-ol, Isoflavonoid. This chapter summarizes the concept of Flavonoids and sources of Flavonoids for preventing metabolic disorders like obesity and diabetes.

Keywords: Flavonoids, socio-economic status, metabolic disorder

1. Introduction

Obesity is a condition that results in weight gain by an increase in excessive body fat. More than 300 million people are categorized as obese who have more than 30 kg/m2 body mass index by International Obesity Taskforce. Obesity develops by various factors such as sedentary lifestyle, socio-economic status, genetic factors, processed food and more involvement in television, games, video, diet pattern, environment as home, workplace. With the increasing rate of obesity, Obesity is accompanied by complex diseases such as enhanced oxidative stress, increased inflammatory marker expression and insulin resistance and type 2 diabetes, sleep apnea, gallbladder disease, cardiovascular disease (CVD), cancer as breast, endometrial, colon, prostate and kidney, osteoarthritis, hypertension. Obesity can be prevented in various ways as surgical methods, a healthy diet, physical exercise, and natural dietary constituents can regulate fat deposition and help to maintain body weight.

2. Flavonoids

Flavonoids or bioflavonoids are the most abundant and secondary metabolites of plants in the human diet. It is taken from the Latin word flavus meaning yellow. Over chemical treatments, more than 5000 naturally occurring Flavonoids have beneficial effects. Flavonoids modulate oxidative stress by act as antioxidants and also helps in cardiovascular diseases, obesity, diabetes, and other age related diseases. Flavonoids are divided into six major subgroups such as Anthocyanins (including cyanidin, delphinidin, malvidin, pelargonidin, peonidin, and petunidin)

1) Flavonols (including quercetin, kaempferol, and myricetin),
2) flavones (including apigenin and luteolin)
3) Flavanones (including eriodictyol, hesperetin, and naringenin),
4) flavans-3-ol (including catechin)
5) Isoflavonoids (including daidzein, genistein, and glycitein)

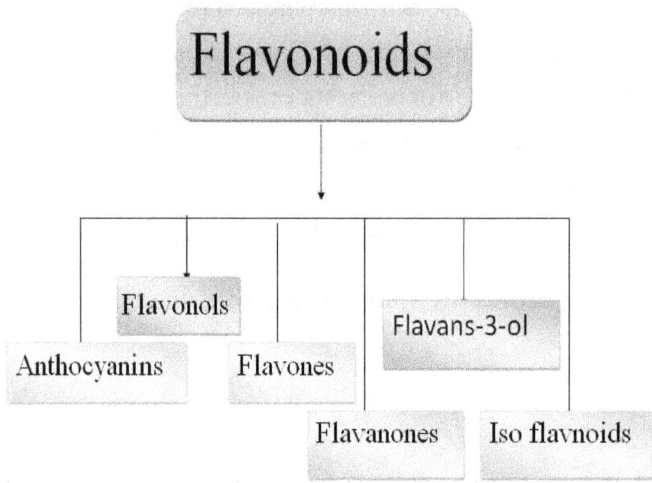

Fig 1. Classification of Flavanoids

2.1 Anthocyanins

In the human diet, Flavonoids are found in rich amounts as in fruits, vegetables, and red wine. It is water insoluble, the pigment in purple brinjal. Due to the predominance of anthocyanins, cherries, red grapes, rhododendron flowers, blueberries achieve their color appeal. There are 635 compounds in nature such as petunidin, cyaniding, malvidin, and peonidin. Anthocyanins have its beneficial effects as an antioxidant, anti-diabetic, anti-inflammatory and anti-obesity. cyanidin 3- glucoside have very therapeutic implications for anti-obesity as it helps in the improvement of leptin and adiponectin secretion.

2.2 Flavonols

In-plant kingdom, flavonols are the most abundant Flavonoids. It includes fisetin, isorhamnetin, quercetin, kaempferol and myricetin. Quercetin helps to lower body weight, decrease blood pressure and reduction of hyperglycemia. Kaempferol acts as anti-diabetic as it helps to reduce hyperglycemia. It is rich in apples, tea, potatoes, and spinach. Myricetin is the third type of flavanols that shows beneficial effects in anti-diabetic and anti-obesity which can be obtained from wine, tea, and fruits and berries.

2.3 Flavones

Apigenin and luteolin are two dietary types of flavones. Apginenin is found in chamomile which is further used in diseases as medications and luteolin is present in cabbage, parsley, celery e.t.c. which acts as anti-diabetic and anti-obesity.

2.4 Flavanones

Flavanones such as Naringenin and Hesperidin are present in citrus fruit as tomatoes, grapes that have various properties as lipid-lowering, anti-diabetic, antioxidant and anti-inflammatory effects. Hesperidin helps to improvement in hyperglycemia and in the regulation of hepatic glucose metabolism. Eriodictyol is also other flavones that help in anti-obesity, and anti-diabetes which is also found in citrus fruits such as lemon, grapes.

2.5 Flavan-3-ols

It is found in tea, cocoa, and chocolates catechin and epicatechin are present in fruits and cocoa. While, epicatechingallate (ECG), gallocatechin, epigallocatechin (EGC), epigallocatechin gallate (EGCG) are found in grapes, tea which helps to control obesity and diabetes. It has been seen that daily intake of EGCG or green tea helps to prevent cardiovascular disease and increase energy expenditure by suppressing dietary lipid absorption.

2.6 Isoflavones

Isoflavones can be obtained from soybean and soy products such as daidzein and genistein. Various studies have been shown that Isoflavones have a positive effect on lipid metabolism, glucose homeostasis, insulin secretion.

Table 1: Beneficial effect of Flavonoids

Flavonoids	Sources	Beneficial Effects
Anthocyanins	Fruit, vegetables, Red wine, cherries, red grapes, rhododendron flowers and blueberries	Anti-oxidant, Anti- diabetic, anti-inflammatory and anti-obesity
Flavonols	Apple, tea, potato, spinach, wines, tea, and fruits	Decrease blood pressure, hyperglycemia, anti-obesity
Flavones	Chamomile, cabbage, parsley, celery	anti- diabetic and anti- obesity
Flavanones	citrus fruit as tomatoes, grapes	lipid-lowering anti-diabetic, anti-oxidant and anti-inflammatory effects
Flavan-3-ols	tea, cocoa, and chocolates	increase energy expenditure by suppressing dietary lipid absorption cardiovascular disease
Isoflavones	soybean and soy products	hyperinsulinemia, and hyperlipidemia, glucose homeostasis

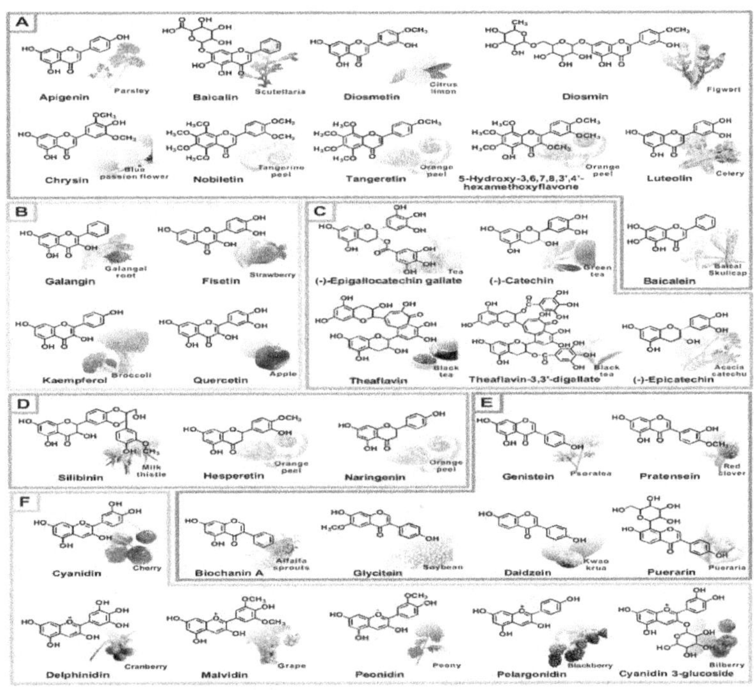

Fig 2. Flavonoids and its Sources

Conclusion

Due to the increased prevalence of obesity and its comorbidities, several drugs and non-drug product has been introduced in the market for preventing and management of weight loss. With this, natural products have emerging trends in the world of pesticide foods such as Flavonoids. Thus, various studies have shown the effect of natural products in combating anti-obesity and anti-diabetes. So, there are various types of Flavonoids which have shown the effect on lowering lipid metabolism, anti-oxidant, anti-diabetes, increasing energy expenditure, glucose homeostasis. So, Flavonoids can be used as safe and efficacious for combating the metabolic disorders.

References

1. Ferreira, I.M., Verreschi, I.T., Nery, L.E., Goldstein, R.S., Zamel, N., Brooks, D. & Jardim, J.R. (1998). The influence of 6 months of oral anabolic steroids on body mass and respiratory muscles in undernourished COPD patients. Chest, 114, 19–28
2. Sharma, N.K.; Ahirwar, D.; Jhade, D.; Jain, V.K. In-vitro anti-obesity assay of alcoholic and aqueous extracts of camellia sinensis leaves. Int. J. Pharm. Sci. Res. 2012, 3, 1863–1866.

3. Pi-Sunyer, F.X. (1991). Health implications of obesity. American Journal of Clinical Nutrition, 53, 1595S–1603S.

4. Willett,W.C.,Dietz,W.H.& Colditz,G.A.(199).Guidelines for healthy weight. The New England Journal of Medicine, 341, 427–434

5. Shari, S. & Bassuk, J.E.M. (2006). Overview of the obesity epidemic and its relationship to cardiovascular disease. In: Obesity and Cardiovascular Disease. Robinson, M.K. & Thomas A. (eds), Taylor & Francis, New York, pp. 1–32.

6. Prasad, S.; Phromnoi, K.; Yadav, V.R.; Chaturvedi, M.M.; Aggarwal, B.B. Targeting inflammatory pathways by flavonoids for prevention and treatment of cancer. PlantaMed. 2010, 76, 1044–1063.

7. Castellarin, S.D.; Di Gaspero, G. Transcriptional control of anthocyanin biosynthetic genes in extreme phenotypes for berry pigmentation of naturally occurring grapevines. BMCPlantBiol. 2007,7,46.

8. Jayaprakasam, B.; Olson, L.K.; Schutzki, R.E.; Tai, M.H.; Nair, M.G. Amelioration of obesity and glucose intolerance in high-fat-fed c57bl/6 mice by anthocyanins and ursolic acid in cornelian cherry (cornus mas). J. Agric. Food Chem. 2006, 54, 243–248

9. Lee, E.R.; Kang, Y.J.; Choi, H.Y.; Kang, G.H.; Kim, J.H.; Kim, B.W.; Han, Y.S.; Nah, S.Y.; Paik, H.D.; Park, Y.S.; et al. Induction of apoptotic cell death by synthetic naringenin derivatives in human lung epithelial carcinoma a549 cells. Biol. Pharm. Bull. 2007, 30, 2394–2398.

10. Havsteen, B.H. The biochemistry and medical significance of the flavonoids. Pharmacol. Ther. 2002, 96, 67–202.

11. Prasain, J.; Carlson, S.; Wyss, J. Flavonoids and age-related disease: Risk, benefits and critical windows. Maturitas 2010, 66, 163–171.

12. Kumar, S.; Gupta, A.; Pandey, A.K. Calotropis procera root extract has the capability to combat free radical mediated damage. ISRN Pharmacol. 2013.

13. Cook, N.; Samman, S. Flavonoids—chemistry, metabolism, cardioprotective effects, and dietary sources. J. Nutr. Biochem. 1996, 7, 66–76.

14. Rice-evans, C.A.; Miller, N.J.; Bolwell, P.G.; Bramley, P.M.; Pridham, J.B. The relative antioxidant activities of plant-derived polyphenolic flavonoids. Free Radic. Res. 1995, 22, 375–383.

15. Middleton, E., Jr. Effect of Plant Flavonoids on Immune and Inflammatory Cell Function; Springer: Berlin, Germany, 1998; pp. 175–182.

16. Takikawa, M.; Inoue, S.; Horio, F.; Tsuda, T. Dietary anthocyanin-rich bilberry extract ameliorates hyperglycemia and insulin sensitivity via activation of AMP-activated protein kinase in diabetic mice. J. Nutr. 2010, 140, 527–533.

17. Ghosh, D.; Konishi, T. Anthocyanins and anthocyanin-rich extracts: Role in diabetes and eye function. Asia Pac. J. Clin. Nutr. 2007, 16, 200.

18. Galvano, F.; La Fauci, L.; Vitaglione, P.; Fogliano, V.; Vanella, L.; Felgines, C. Bioavailability, antioxidant and biological properties of the natural free-radical scavengers cyanidin and related glycosides. Ann. Ist. Super. Sanita 2007, 43, 382–393.

19. Dai, X.Q.; Ding, Y.; Zhang, Z.F.; Cai, X.X.; Li, Y. Quercetin and quercitrin protect against cytokine-induced injuries in RINm5F β-cells via the mitochondrial pathway and NF-κB signaling. Int. J. Mol. Med. 2013, 31, 265–271.

20. Tsuda, T.; Ueno, Y.; Yoshikawa, T.; Kojo, H.; Osawa, T. Microarray profiling of gene expression in human adipocytes in response to anthocyanins. Biochem. Pharmacol. 2006, 71, 1184–1197.

21. Crozier, A.; Jaganath, I.B.; Clifford, M.N. Dietary phenolics: Chemistry, bioavailability and effects on health. Nat. Prod. Rep. 2009, 26, 1001–1043.

22. Edwards, R.L.; Lyon, T.; Litwin, S.E.; Rabovsky, A.; Symons, J.D.; Jalili, T. Quercetin reduces blood pressure in hypertensive subjects. J. Nutr. 2007, 137, 2405–2411

23. Yamamoto, Y.; Oue, E. Antihypertensive effect of quercetin in rats fed with a high-fat high-sucrose diet. Biosci. Biotechnol. Biochem. 2006, 70, 933–939.

24. Fang, X.K.; Gao, J.; Zhu, D.N. Kaempferol and quercetin isolated from euonymus alatus improve glucose uptake of 3T3-L1 cells without adipogenesis activity. Life Sci. 2008, 82, 615–622.

25. Rivera,L.;Morón,R.;Sánchez,M.;Zarzuelo,A.;Galisteo,M.Quercetin ameliorates metabolic syndrome and improves the inflammatory status in obese zucker rats. Obesity 2008, 16, 2081–2087.

26. Jorge, A.P.; Horst, H.; de Sousa, E.; Pizzolatti, M.G.; Silva, F.R. Insulinomimetic effects of kaempferitrin on glycaemia and on 14c-glucose uptake in rat soleus muscle. Chem. Biol. Interact. 2004, 149, 89–96.

27. Häkkinen,S.H.;Kärenlampi,S.O.;Heinonen,I.M.;Mykkänen,H.M.;Törrönen,A.R.Contentof theflavonols quercetin, myricetin, and kaempferolin 25 edible berries. J.Agric. FoodChem. 1999,47,2274–2279.

28. Nirmala, P.; Ramanathan, M. Effect of kaempferol on lipid peroxidation and antioxidant status in 1,2-dimethyl hydrazine induced colorectal carcinoma in rats. Eur. J. Pharmacol. 2011, 654, 75–79.

29. Hiermann, A.; Schramm, H.; Laufer, S. Anti-inflammatory activity of myricetin-3-O-β-D-glucuronide and related compounds. Inflamm. Res. 1998, 47, 421–427.

30. Hertog, M.G.; Hollman, P.C.; van de Putte, B. Content of potentially anticarcinogenic flavonoids of tea infusions, wines, and fruit juices. J. Agric. Food Chem. 1993, 41, 1242–1246.

31. Neuhouser, M.L. Dietary flavonoids and cancer risk: Evidence from human population studies. Nutr. Cancer 2004, 50, 1–7.

32. Miean, K.H.; Mohamed, S. Flavonoid (myricetin, quercetin, kaempferol, luteolin, and apigenin) content of edible tropical plants. J. Agric. Food Chem. 2001, 49, 3106–3112.

33. Gates,M.A.;Tworoger,S.S.;Hecht,J.L.;deViv, I.; Rosner, B.; Hankinson, S.E.A prospective study of dietary flavonoid intake and incidence of epithelial ovarian cancer. Int. J. Cancer 2007, 121, 2225–2232.

34. Choe, S.C.; Kim, H.S.; Jeong, T.S.; Bok, S.H.; Park, Y.B. Naringin has an antiatherogenic effect with the inhibition of intercellular adhesion molecule-1 in hypercholesterolemic rabbits. J. Cardiovasc. Pharmacol. 2001, 38, 947–955.

35. Hasanein, P.; Fazeli, F. Role of naringenin in protection against diabetic hyperalgesia and tactile allodynia in male wistar rats. J. Physiol. Biochem. 2014, 70, 997–1006.

36. Jung,U.J.Lee,M.-K.;Jeong,K.S.;Choi,M.S.The hypoglycaemic effects of hesperidin and naringin are partly mediated by hepatic glucose-regulating enzymes in C57BL/KsJ-db/db mice. J.Nutr. 2004, 134, 2499–2503.

37. Kim, H.J.; Oh, G.T.; Park, Y.B.; Lee, M.K.; Seo, H.J.; Choi, M.S. Naringin alters the cholesterol biosynthesis and antioxidant enzyme activities in ldl receptor-knockout mice under cholesterol fed condition. Life Sci. 2004, 74, 1621–1634.

38. Zygmunt, K.; Faubert, B.; MacNeil, J.; Tsiani, E. Naringenin, a citrus flavonoid, increases muscle cell glucose uptake via ampk. Biochem. Biophys. Res. Commun. 2010, 398, 178–183. [CrossRef] [PubMed]

39. Goldwasser, J.; Cohen, P.Y.; Yang, E.; Balaguer, P.; Yarmush, M.L.; Nahmias, Y. Transcriptional regulation of human and rat hepatic lipid metabolism by the grape fruit flavonoid naringenin: RoleofPPARα,PPARγ and LXRα. PLoS ONE 2010, 5, e12399.

40. Jung, U.J.; Kim, H.J.; Lee, J.S.; Lee, M.K.; Kim, H.O.; Park, E.J.; Kim, H.K.; Jeong, T.S.; Choi, M.S. Naringin supplementation lowers plasma lipids and enhances erythrocyte antioxidant enzyme activities in hypercholesterolemic subjects. Clin. Nutr. 2003, 22, 561–568.

41. Jung, U.J.; Choi, M.-S. Obesity and its metabolic complications: The role of adipokines and the relationship between obesity, inflammation, insulin resistance, dyslipidemia and nonalcoholic fatty liver disease. Int. J. Mol. Sci. 2014, 15, 6184–6223.

42. Zhang, W.-Y.; Lee, J.-J.; Kim, Y.; Kim, I.-S.; Han, J.-H.; Lee, S.-G.; Ahn, M.-J.; Jung, S.-H.; Myung, C.-S. Effect of eriodictyol on glucose uptake and insulin resistance in vitro. J. Agric. Food Chem. 2012, 60, 7652–7658.

43. Yang, C.S.; Chen, L.; Lee, M.-J.; Balentine, D.; Kuo, M.C.; Schantz, S.P. Blood and urine levels of tea catechins after ingestion of different amounts of green tea by human volunteers. Cancer Epidemiol. Biomark. Prev. 1998, 7, 351–354.

44. Sartippour, M.R.; Shao, Z.-M.; Heber, D.; Beatty, P.; Zhang, L.; Liu, C.; Ellis, L.; Liu, W.; Go, V.L.; Brooks, M.N. Green tea inhibits vascular endothelial growth factor (VEGF) induction in human breast cancer cells. J. Nutr. 2002, 132, 2307–2311.

45. Kavanagh, K.T.; Hafer, L.J.; Kim, D.W.; Mann, K.K.; Sherr, D.H.; Rogers, A.E.; Sonenshein, G.E. Green tea extracts decrease carcinogen-induced mammary tumor burden in rats and rate of breast cancer cell proliferation in culture. J. Cell. Biochem. 2001, 82, 387–398.

46. Osada, K.; Takahashi, M.; Hoshina, S.; Nakamura, M.; Nakamura, S.; Sugano, M. Tea catechins inhibit cholesterol oxidation accompanying oxidation of low density lipoprotein in vitro. Comp. Biochem. Physiol. C 2001, 128, 153–164.

47. Kao, Y.H.; Hiipakka, R.A.; Liao, S. Modulation of endocrine systems and food intake by green tea epigallocatechin gallate. Endocrinology 2000, 141, 980–987.

48. Wolfram, S. Effects of green tea and egcg on cardiovascular and metabolic health. J. Am. Coll. Nutr. 2007, 26, 373S–388S.

49. Hsu, T.F.; Kusumoto, A.; Abe, K.; Hosoda, K.; Kiso, Y.; Wang, M.F.; Yamamoto, S. Polyphenol-enriched oolong tea increases fecal lipid excretion. Eur. J. Clin. Nutr. 2006, 60, 1330–1336.

50. Park, H.-Y.; Kim, M.; Han, J. Stereospecific microbial production of isoflavanones from isoflavones and isoflavone glucosides. Appl. Microbiol. Biotechnol. 2011, 91, 1173–1181.

Chapter-2

ANTIOXIDANTS AND THEIR ROLE IN NUTRITION

Vijeta Goyal

*Department of Foods and Nutrition,
Government Home Science College, Punjab University, Chandigarh, India*

ABSTRACT

Antioxidants are natural or man-made a substance that delays or prevent damage to the cells caused by free radicals. Researchers have shown that people who consume raw food like fruits and vegetables are at lower risk of developing a disease like cancer, cardiovascular diseases, cataracts, and various brain dysfunctions. Diet high in fruits, vegetables, nuts, and oilseeds provides a good source of antioxidants. Some oxidants are manufactured by our body and some need to be obtained from the food. The antioxidants such as Vitamin A, Vitamin C, Vitamin E, Carotenoids and phytochemicals which are abundantly present in the food reduces the oxidative stress caused by free radicals. Antioxidants help protect our body against foreign particles, thus enhancing the Immune system.

Keywords: Antioxidants, Vitamin A, Vitamin C, Carotenoids, Phytochemicals, Free Radicals.

1. Introduction

As humans, we all face stress and living with it is normal in today's fast-paced life. The short term stress is normal as it helps to stay focused and helps to meet the daily challenges at the workplace and in daily life. If the body is under continuous stress like long working hours, less sleep, traveling for hours, tight deadlines are deteriorating both physical and mental health. The body relies on antioxidants to reduce or delay the cell damage caused by "free radicals" and other supplements. The body when exposed to free radicals through various environmental sources, such as cigarette smoke, air pollution, and sunlight, attack the healthy cells resulting alteration in the cell structure and function (oxidative stress), which can lead to health-related diseases like cancer, diabetes, cardiovascular diseases, Parkinson's disease, Alzheimer's disease and certain eye-related diseases.

2. Antioxidants and their types

The role of Antioxidants in certain diseases is of growing interest to food scientists and other health professionals due to their protective roles against oxidative deterioration in the body. Antioxidant plays a very important role in building the defense system of the body. Antioxidants are substances that blunt the action of free radicals. In other term, antioxidants are any substance that delays or inhibits oxidation of that substrate even when present at low concentrations. Nature has provided a unique protective mechanism to every cell against any harmful effects of free radicals such as superoxide dismutase (SOD), glutathione reductase, glutathione peroxidases are the enzymatic antioxidants.

3. Major antioxidants & their sources

The plant-based foods, especially fruits and vegetables, provide the best source of antioxidants. Some foods are extremely nutritionally dense and hence good for once health and are usually referred to as a "superfood" or "functional food." Superfoods or functional foods have large doses of vitamins and minerals that can help to keep the diseases at bay and live a longer, healthier life. To include the benefits of antioxidants, try to include the following in your diet:

3.1 Vitamin A

Bright colored orange-yellow fruits and vegetables (e.g., cantaloupe, carrots, mangoes) and green leafy vegetables, peas.

3.2 Vitamin C

Most fruits and vegetables, especially berries, oranges, bell peppers, guava, amla (gooseberry), pineapple, tomatoes, spinach, carrots.

3.3 Vitamin E

Nuts and seeds, sunflower and other vegetable oils (soybean, safflower and corn oil) and green leafy vegetables.

Lycopene: Pink and red fruits and vegetables, including tomatoes, watermelon, pink grapefruit, pink guava, papaya, seabuckthorn, Goji berries, and rosehip

Lutein: Green leafy vegetables, corn, papaya, and oranges

Selenium: Rice, corn, wheat, nuts, eggs, cheese, turkey, fish, pork, beef, and legumes

Other foods that are good sources of antioxidants are as follows:

- eggplants
- legumes such as black beans or kidney beans

- green and black teas
- red grapes
- dark chocolate
- Pomegranates

Table 1 Antioxidants sources

Adapted from the International Food Information Council Foundation: Media Guide on Food Safety and Nutrition: 2004-2006. Not a representation of all sources.

Antioxidant and their sources		
Class/Components	**Source**	**Potential Benefit**
Carotenoids		
Beta-carotene	carrots, sweet potatoes, butternut squash, apricots, spinach, cantaloupe	neutralizes free radicals which may damage cells; supports cellular antioxidant defenses
Lutein, Zeaxanthin	kale, collards, spinach, corn, eggs, citrus fruits	may contribute to the maintenance of healthy vision
Lycopene	tomatoes and processed tomato products	may contribute to the maintenance of prostate health
Flavonoids		
Anthocyanidins	berries, cherries, red grapes	support cellular antioxidant defenses; may contribute to the maintenance of brain function
Flavanols—Catechins, Epicatechins, Procyanidins	tea, cocoa, chocolate, apples, grapes	may contribute to the maintenance of heart health

Flavanones	citrus foods	neutralize free radicals which may damage cells; support cellular antioxidant defenses
Flavonols	onions, apples, tea, broccoli	neutralize free radicals which may damage cells; support cellular antioxidant defenses
Proanthocyanidins	cranberries, cocoa, apples, strawberries, grapes, wine, peanuts, cinnamon	may contribute to the maintenance of urinary tract health and heart health
Isothiocyanates		
Sulforaphane	cauliflower, broccoli, broccoli sprouts, cabbage, kale, horseradish	may enhance detoxification of undesirable compounds and support cellular antioxidant defenses
Phenols		
Caffeic acid, Ferulic acid	apples, pears, citrus fruits, some vegetables	may bolster cellular antioxidant defenses; may contribute to the maintenance of healthy vision and heart health
Sulfides/Thiols		
Diallyl sulfide, Allyl methyl trisulfide	garlic, onions, leeks, scallions	may enhance detoxification of undesirable compounds; may contribute to the maintenance of heart health and healthy immune function
Dithiolethiones	cruciferous vegetables—broccoli, cabbage, bok choy, collard greens	contribute to the maintenance of healthy immune function

Whole Grains		
Whole grains	cereal grains	may reduce the risk of coronary heart disease and cancer; may contribute to a reduced risk of diabetes

Table 2: Examples of Antioxidant Vitamins and Minerals

Chart adapted from the Food and Nutrition Board Institute of Medicine DRI reports and National Institutes of Health Office of Dietary Supplements.

*DRI's provided are a range for Americans ages 2-70.

Vitamins	Daily Reference Intakes*	Antioxidant Activity	Source
Vitamin A	300-900 µg/d	Protects cells from free radicals	Liver, dairy products, fish
Vitamin C	15-90 mg/d	Protects cells from free radicals	Bell peppers, citrus fruits
Vitamin E	6-15 mg/d	Protects cells from free radicals, helps with immune function and DNA repair	Oils, fortified cereals, sunflower seeds, mixed nuts
Selenium	20-55 µg/d	Helps prevent cellular damage from free radicals	Brazil nuts, meats, tuna, plant foods

4. Antioxidants and their role in the prevention of diseases

4.1 Carotenoids

Carotenoids are the plant pigments that provide yellow and orange color to fruits and vegetables. Carotenoids are a group of phytonutrients and have an important antioxidant function which reduces the activity of free radicals — single oxygen atoms that can damage cells by reacting with other molecules. They have strong cancer-fighting properties and help prevent cardiovascular diseases, cancer, and other degenerative diseases. Beta carotene is a fat-soluble vitamin and is converted to vitamin A, which is essential for good vision and normal growth and development in human beings.

4.2 Lycopene

Lycopene is a bright red color pigment responsible for the beautiful color of watermelons, guavas, and grapefruit. Lycopene is a strong antioxidant that reduces the risk of prostate cancer, breast cancer, cervical cancer, and ovarian cancer. A recent study which was published in the Journal of the National Cancer Institute did on nearly 50,000 men, found that prostate cancer risk is less in men with high levels of lycopene. Lycopene promotes bone health, thus, preventing osteoporosis.   Many studies show it has heart-protective properties. Lycopene shows a significant reduction in the levels of oxidized LDL (LDLox) in subjects consuming homemade tomato sauce and tomato juice.   In another small study, lycopene was shown to reduce total serum cholesterol levels and thereby lowering the risk of cardiovascular diseases.

4.3 Polyphenols

Polyphenols are the class of phytochemicals and naturally occurs in the plant kingdom. Recently polyphenols being a matter of interest in many research studies as they prevent damage in the cells from free-radicals that occur from pollution, smoking, eating foods that have turned rancid, and is associated with a lower risk of several chronic diseases. Thus, polyphenols are grouped into four different categories based on their structure: phenolic acids, flavonoids, stilbenes, and lignans.

4.4 Phenolic acids

They are widely found in the skin of fruits and vegetables. Coffee, tea, grapes, red wine, berries, kiwi fruits, plums, apples, and cherries are some of the foods that contain a high amount of phenolic acid.

Phenolic acids are abundantly present in the diet and absorbed in the intestinal tract. Phenolic acids work as antioxidants but also have anti-inflammatory properties. Phenolic acid attributed different biological properties like anti-ulcer, antidepressant activities, antitumor, anti-inflammatory, antispasmodic, antioxidant and cytotoxic. Phenolic acid polymers are known as Tannins. Tannins have anti-inflammatory, antiseptics, and antioxidant properties. The next group is the flavonoids which also include isoflavones found in soy, anthocyanins found in blueberries, cherries, eggplant, prunes and wine, flavones found in black tea, cocoa, buckwheat, and dark chocolate. flavonols found in broccoli and tomato, flavanones are present in citrus fruits, apples, berries and pears, and flavan-3-ols occur in cocoa, tea, and wine. Flavonoids are a group of chemicals widely present in plant-based foods such as fruits, vegetables, legumes, red wine, and green tea. Flavonoids—sometimes called "bioflavonoids" and are often sold as dietary supplements. Dietary flavonoids like epicatechin, gallate, gallic acid, quercetin-3-glucoside possess strong antioxidant activities reported by Salucci et al. Last but not least, some famous polyphenols that don't fit into any class, including resveratrol and stilbenes from wine and nuts, curcumin in spices, and lignans in flaxseeds

5. Vitamin C

Vitamin C is known as Ascorbic acid, which is a water-soluble vitamin. Vitamin C is required for the normal growth and maintenance of the various body tissues, including collagen, which is needed for healthy connective tissue and wound healing. Citrus fruits, strawberries, potatoes, broccoli, oranges, guava, tomatoes, and peppers are the food sources high in vitamin C. Vitamin C also helps in the better absorption of iron from plant sources spinach, nuts, and seeds. Vitamin C also helps to keep the bones and teeth strong. Vitamin C is required for the production of hormones and certain neurotransmitters. This vitamin helps in the detoxification of the liver. Ascorbic acid plays a major role in the proper functioning of the immune system. It acts as an antioxidant and reduces the inflammatory response in the body caused by histamines and peroxide. Its antioxidant property is also known for the reduction of certain cancer incidences

6. Vitamin E

Vitamin E, commonly known as tocopherol. It is a member of a fat-soluble vitamin that includes Vitamin A, Vitamin D, and Vitamin K. It is an important defense antioxidant that protects the body from the free radicals and prevents the blood platelets from sticking together. Natural vitamin E occurs naturally in eight different forms, but alpha-tocopherol is the only form that helps to meet the daily human requirements. Nuts and seeds, edible vegetable oils, cereals, and dark green leafy vegetables are all excellent sources of vitamin E. Deficiency is rare and is caused due to the digestive tract diseases that prevent absorption. Symptoms of Vitamin E deficiency include nerve, muscle and eye problems and a weakened immune system.

The Health and Medicine Division of National Academies of Sciences, Engineering, and Medicine has suggested the dietary reference intakes (DRI) for vitamin E based on age. Pregnant and breastfeeding women do not require extra vitamin E and the daily requirement is met by a balanced diet.

Dietary Reference Intakes
1 to 3 years: 6 milligrams per day
4 to 8 years: 7 milligrams per day
9 to 13 years: 11 milligrams per day
14+ years: 15 milligrams per day

7. Conclusion

There is no doubt that food is information, and Food can act as natural medicine. Antioxidant-rich foods abundantly found in fruits, vegetables, nuts, and seeds are nature's pharmacy to heal the body and keep away the inflammation and disease. Free radicals are responsible and are linked to various diseases including heart disease, cancer, and vision loss. Antioxidants from natural or manmade sources reduce the risk of certain diseases if followed by a healthy and balanced diet. The major source of antioxidants is plant food. Indian spices, fruits, vegetables, and herbs are rich sources of natural antioxidants. These are present in sufficient amounts to meet the daily requirement. High levels of antioxidants are used in the development of functional food and are gaining importance as they may play disease preventive role for mankind.

References

1. https://nccih.nih.gov/health/antioxidants/introduction.htm
2. Halliwell, B. 2007. Biochemistry of oxidative stress. Biochem. Soc. Trans. 35, 1147-1150.
3. Khlebnikov, A. I., Schepetkin, I. A., Domina,N. G., Kirpotina, L. N., Quinn, M. T. 2007. Improved quantitative structure-activity relationship models to predict antioxidant activity of flavonoids in chemical, enzymatic, and cellular systems. Bioorg. Med. Chem.15, 1749-1770.
4. Halliwell, B. 1990. How to characterize a biological antioxidant. Free Radic. Res.Commun. 9, 1-32
5. Sies H. (ed.) Antioxidants in Disease, Mechanisms and Therapy, Academic Press, New York, 1996.
6. Ames BN. Dietary carcinogens and anticarcinogens, oxygen radicals and degenerative diseases. Science, 1983, 221:1256–1264.
7. Moncada S, Higgs EA. Mechanisms of disease: the L-arginine-nitric oxide pathway. New England Journal of Medicine, 1993, 329:2002–2012.
8. Sies H. (ed.) Antioxidants in Disease, Mechanisms and Therapy, Academic Press, New York, 1996.
9. Cadenas E and Packer L, (eds) Handbook of Antioxidants. Plenum Publishers, New York, 1996.
10. Vivekananthan DP, Penn MS, Sapp SK, et al. Use of antioxidant vitamins for the prevention of cardiovascular disease: meta analysis of randomized trials. The Lancet 2003; 361:2017-23.
11. Bagchi K and Puri S. Free radicals and antioxidants in health and disease. Eastern Mediterranean Health Journal.1998; 4: 350-360.

12. Beecher G. Overview of dietary flavonoids: nomenclature, occurrence and intake. J Nutr.2003; 133: 3248S–3254S.

13. Antioxidants and Cancer Prevention: Fact Sheet. National Cancer Institute. 2007; 2: 27.

14. Ortega RM. Importance of functional foods in the Mediterranean diet. Public Health Nutr.2006; 9: 1136–40. Breton F. Which wines have the most health benefits? 2008.(http://www.frenchscout.com/polyphenols)

15. Mangels AR, Holden JM, Beecher GR, Forman MR, Lanza E. Carotenoid contents of fruits and vegetables: an evaluation of analytical data. J Am Diet Assoc 1993;93:284–96.

16. The National Cancer Institute (http://www.cancer.gov/newscenter/pressreleases/antioxidants/)

17. Efficacy of antioxidant supplementation in reducing primary cancer incidence and mortality: Systematic review and meta-analysis. (Jan. 2008). *Mayo Clinic Proceedings, 83*,1, 23-34.

18. Johnson EJ. The role of carotenoids in human health. Nutr Clin Care 2002;5(2):47–9.

19. Agarwal S, Rao AV. Carotenoids and chronic diseases. Drug Metab Drug Interact 2000;17(1–4):189–210.

20. Paiva S, Russell R. Beta carotene and other carotenoids as antioxidants. J Am Coll, Nutr1999; 18:426–33.

21. Astrog P, Gradelet S, Berges R, Suschetet M. Dietary lycopene decreases initiation of liver preneoplastic foci by diethylnitrosamine in rat. Nutr Cancer 1997;29:60–8.

22. Lien, A.P., H. Hua and P. Chuong, 2008. Free radicals, antioxidants in disease and health. Int. J. Biomed. Sci., (4)2: 89-96.

23. Paiva S, Russell R. Beta carotene and other carotenoids as antioxidants. J Am Coll, Nutr 1999; 18:426–33.

24. Stahl W, Sies H. Lycopene: a biologically important carotenoid for humans? Arch Biochem Biophys 1996;336:1–9.

25. Giovannucci E. Tomatoes, tomato-based products, lycopene, and cancer: review of the epidemiologic literature. J Natl Cancer Inst 1999; 91:317–31.Arab L, Steck S. Lycopene and cardiovascular disease. Am J Clin Nutr 2000;71(suppl):1691S–5S.

26. Rissanen T. Lycopene and cardiovascular disease. In: Rao AV, editor, Tomatoes,lycopene and human health. Scotland: Caledonian Science Press; 2006. p. 141–52.

27. Rissanen T, Vontilainen S, Nyyssonen K, Salonen R, Salonen JT. Low plasma lycopene concentration is associated with increased intima-media thickness of the carotid artery wall. Arteriocler Thromb Vasc Biol 2000; 20:2677–87.

28. USDA's Database on the Flavonoid Content

29. Oomah, B. Dave; Mazza, Giuseppe (1996). "Flavonoids and Antioxidative Activities in Buckwheat". *Journal of Agricultural and Food Chemistry*. **44** (7): 1746–1750. doi:10.1021/jf9508357.

30. Witztum JL. The oxidation hypothesis of atherosclerosis. Lancet 1994; 344:793–6.

31. Parthasarathy S, Steinberg D, Witztum JL. The role of oxidized low density lipoproteins in pathogenesis of atherosclerosis. Ann Rev Med 1992; 43:219–25.

32. Heller FR, Descamps O, Hondekijn JC. LDL oxidation: therapeutic perspectives.Atherosclerosis 1998; 137:S25–31.

33. Agarwal S, Rao AV. Tomato lycopene and low density lipoprotein oxidation: a human dietary intervention study. Lipids 1998; 33:981–4.

34. Fuhramn B, Elis A, Aviram M. Hypocholesterolemic effect of lycopene and b-carotene is related to suppression of cholesterol synthesis and augmentation of LDL receptor activity in macrophage. Biochem Biophys Res Commun 1997; 233:658–62.

35. Bohn T. (2010). Isoflavone bioavailability from foods and supplements. Dietary factors impacting utilization. Agro Food Industry Hi-Tech; 21, 59-62

36. Bouayed, J. (2010). Polyphenols: a potential new strategy for the prevention and treatment of anxiety and depression. Curr Nutr Food Sci, 6, 13-18.

37. Manach C, Scalbert A, Morand C, Remesy C, Jimenez L. Polyphenols: food sources and bioavailability. American Jour Clinical Nut. 79, 2004; 727–747.

38. Pietta PG, Rice-Evans CA, Packer L. Flavonoids in Health and Disease. Marcel Dekker New York. 23, 1998; 61–110.

39. Kukic J, Petrovic S, Niketic M. Antioxidant activity of four endemic Stachys taxa. Biol Pharmaceut Bull. 29, 2006; 725-729.

40. Tiwari AK. Imbalance in antioxidant defence and human disease: multiple approach of natural antioxidants therapy. Current Science. 81, 2001; 1179-1187.

41. Lupulescu A Hormones and Vitamins in Cancer Treatment. 1990;149-211, CRC 2.Press, BOCA Ration, Boston.

42. Lupulescu A The Role of Vitamins A, B Carotene, E and C in Cancer Cell Biology. Intern. Vit. Nutr. Res. 1993; 63:3-14.

43. Jemal A, Bray F, Center MM, et al. Global cancer statistics. CA Cancer J Clin. 2011;61:69–90. [PubMed]

44. Salonen JT, Salonen RM, Thanainen M, Parviainen R, Sepparen M, Kantola K. Jeng KC, Yang CS, Siu WY, Tsai YS, Liao WJ & Kuo JS (1996) Supplementation with vitamin C and E enhances cytokine production by peripheral blood mononuclear cells in healthy adults. Am J Clin Nutr 64, 960–965.

45. Haertel C, Strunk T, Bucsky P & Schultz C (2004) Effects of vitamin C on intracytoplasmic cytokine production in human whole blood monocytes and lymphocytes. Cytokine 27, 101–106

46. Handan, M., K. Suleyman, M. Nihat and D. Yeter, 2007. Vitamin status in yearling rams with growth failure. Turk. J. Vet. Anim. Sci., 31(6): 407-409.

47. Paul, W.S. and S. Sumit, 2002. Antioxidants in dietary oils: Their potential role in breast cancer prevention. Mal. J. Nutr., 8(1): 1-11

48. Abdalla, A.E., 2009. The role of antioxidant (Vitamin E) in the control of lead pollution and enhancement of growth within nile tilapia (Oreochromis niloticus). Intern. J. Appl. Res. Vet. Med., 3(7): 97-101.

49. Bashir, M.R., M.H. Guido, J.F.V. Wim and B. Aalt, 2004. The extraordinary antioxidant activity of vitamin E phosphate. Bioch. Biophy. Acta, 1683: 16-21

50. Chem. Soc., 87(3): 295-304. DOI: 10.1007/s11746-009-1497-x.

51. Vivek, K.G. and K.S. Surendra, 2006. Plants as natural antioxidants. Natur. Prod.Radia., 5(4): 326-334.

52. Sarvajeet, S.G. and T. Narendra, 2010. Reactive oxygen species and antioxidant machinery in abiotic stress tolerance in crop plants. Plant Physiol. Bioch., 48: 909-930. Doi:10.1016/j.plaphy.2010.08.016.

Chapter-3

PROBIOTICS AND PREBIOTICS

Shagun Sharma
Maharishi Markandeshwar University, Mullana (Ambala), Haryana, India

and

Disha
I.K Gujral Punjab Technical University, Ibban, Punjab, India

ABSTRACT

Probiotics are live microbes that help in digestion by balancing the intestinal microflora, can be formulated into many different types of products, including foods, drugs, and dietary supplements. Species of *lactobacillus, Bifidobacterium* are most commonly used as probiotics, but the yeast *Saccharomyces cerevisiae* and some *E.coli and Bacillus* species are also used as probiotics. Lactic acid bacteria, including *Lactobacillus* species, which have been used for preservation of food by fermentation for thousands of years, can serve a dual function by acting as agents for food fermentation and in addition potentially imparting health benefits. On the other hand, Prebiotics are the dietary substances (mostly consisting of non-starch polysaccharides and oligosaccharides poorly digested by human enzymes) that nurture a selected group of microorganisms living in the gut. They favor the growth of beneficial bacteria over that of harmful ones. prebiotics are the source of food for the gut microflora, thus helping indigestion.

Keywords: Prebiotic, probiotic, microflora, *Lactobacillus* species.

Probiotics

Introduction

Nowadays the eating habits of the population are changing as the living style is also changing. People are attracted more towards junk food and ready to eat food. The junk food and the food which is not prepared at home contain inappropriate amounts of spices and food preservatives, which may pose harm to the gut. Probiotics here play an important role in helping the digestion of food. Probiotics are living microorganisms that help the intestinal flora indigestion. The gut flora affected by some antibiotics or food can be balanced by probiotics. Almost all the food nutrients are absorbed in the intestine; the probiotics help the intestinal flora in the absorption of the nutrients.

Probiotics can be defined as the alive microbial feed supplements provided in the form of solid food or drink to the human body to improve the function of intestinal flora and the intestinal microbial balance.

History

Probiotics and their considerable powers were revealed when the Roman naturalist **Pliny the Elder** used fermented milk to treat intestinal problems. It was a natural remedy but the reason behind its remedial properties was not known. In the late 1800s, scientist **Ilya Mechnikov** observed that rural people in Bulgaria, in spite of extreme poverty and harsh climates, had average life spans longer than those in wealthy European populations. Mechnikov noted that their diets were rich in yogurt and other fermented milk products. Mechnikov's worked at the Pasteur Institute in Paris where he reinforced his theories on the benefits of lactic acid bacteria produced by  fermentation. Mechnikov and his colleagues were so convinced that they began drinking sour milk, thereby introducing the modern probiotic, which means "for life." Around the same time, another important discovery was made at the **Pasteur Institute** by Henri Tissier who isolated *bifidobacterium* from the gut flora of breast-fed infants. These bacteria, he observed, could lessen diarrhea in babies. For the next several decades, an exploration into probiotics moved slowly. But as a new century approached, probiotics research with randomized, controlled clinical studies soared, showing .e World Health Organization's (WHO) **definition of probiotics**, issued in 2001 is as follows: "live microorganisms which when administered in adequate amounts confer a beneficial health effect on the host." History of probiotics can also be traced to the use of fermented dairy products. Clostridium which is a proteolytic bacteria and is a part of gut microbiota produces a complex substance like phenols, indols, and ammonia by the digestion of proteins. According to Metchnikoff, these compounds were responsible for what he called intestinal autointoxication which causes physical changes in old age. The term "probiotic" refers to microorganisms that affect other organisms. The conception of the proteins involved notion that substances secreted by one microorganism, stimulated the growth of other microorganisms. The term was used to describe tissue extract that stimulated microbial growth. The term was taken up by "Parker", he defined the concept as "organisms and substances that have a beneficial effect on the host animal by contributing to its intestinal microbial balance. Again the term was improved by Fuller, he described probiotics as ``alive microbial feed supplement which positively affects the host animal by improving the intestinal microbial balance. ``

Factors affecting the intestinal micro-ecosystem

- Antibiotics and another drug intake
- Microbial infections
- Diet (highly processed, low fiber foods)
- Chronic diarrhea
- Stress
- Chlorinated water
- Radiation and chemotherapy
- Colonic therapies for detoxification

Mode of action

1. **Probiotics interact with mucosal cells causing their activation:** Adhesion to intestinal mucosa is regarded as a prerequisite for colonization and is important for the interaction between probiotic strains and the host. Adhesion of probiotics to the intestinal mucosa is also important for modulation of the immune system and antagonism against pathogens. Thus, adhesion has been one of the main selection criteria for new probiotic strains and has been related to certain beneficial effects of probiotics. Lactic acid bacteria (LABs) display various surface determinants that are involved in their interaction with intestinal epithelial cells (IECs) and mucus. IECs secrete mucin, which is a complex glycoprotein mixture that is the principal component of mucous, thereby preventing the adhesion of pathogenic bacteria. Additionally, lipids, free proteins, immunoglobulins, and salts are present in mucus gel. This specific interaction has indicated a possible association between the surface proteins of probiotic bacteria and the competitive exclusion of pathogens from the mucus. As mentioned above, several Lactobacillus proteins have been shown to promote mucus adhesion, and bacteria display surface adhesions that mediate attachment to the mucous layer. This process is mainly mediated by proteins, although saccharide moieties and lipoteichoic acids have also been implicated.

2. **Enhance epithelial cell barrier function:** The intestinal epithelium is in permanent contact with luminal contents and the variable, dynamic enteric flora. The intestinal barrier is a major defense mechanism used to maintain epithelial integrity and to protect the organism from the environment. Defenses of the intestinal barrier consist of the mucous layer, antimicrobial peptides, secretory IgA and epithelial junction adhesion complex. Once this barrier function is disrupted, bacterial and food antigens can reach the submucosa and can induce inflammatory responses, which may result in intestinal disorders, such as inflammatory

bowel disease. Consumption of non-pathogenic bacteria can contribute to intestinal barrier function, and probiotic bacteria have been extensively studied for their involvement in the maintenance of this barrier. However, the mechanisms by which probiotics enhance intestinal barrier function are not fully understood.

3. **Proliferation and regulation of t-cells:** It is well known that probiotic bacteria can exert an immunomodulatory effect. These bacteria have the ability to interact with epithelial and dendritic cells (DCs) and with monocytes/macrophages and lymphocytes. The immune system can be divided between the innate and adaptive systems. The adaptive immune response depends on B and T lymphocytes, which are specific for particular antigens. In contrast, the innate immune system responds to common structures called pathogen-associated molecular patterns (PAMPs) shared by the vast majority of pathogens. The primary response to pathogens is triggered by pattern recognition receptors (PPRs), which bind PAMPs. The best-studied PPRs are toll-like receptors (TLRs). In addition, extracellular C-type lectin receptors (CLRs) and intracellular nucleotide-binding oligomerization domain-containing protein (NOD)-like receptors (NLRs) are known to transmit signals upon interaction with bacteria.

Characteristics of Effective Probiotics

- Able to survive the passage through the digestive system.

- Able to attach to the intestinal epithelia and colonize.
- Able to maintain good viability.
- Able to utilize the nutrients and substrates in a normal diet.
- Non-pathogenic and non-toxic.
- Capable of exerting a beneficial effect on the host.
- Stability of desired characteristics during processing, storage, and transportation.
- Anti-inflammatory, anti-mutagenic

Forms: probiotics are available in the form of food supplements, drinks, yogurt, etc.

Dosage forms for the military:

- Standard forms:
    - Capsules
    - Sticks
    - Powder blends
    - Chewable tablets

- Individual customization:

- Capsules
- Sticks
- Chewable tablets
- Sachets
- Tablets

Advantages and disadvantages of probiotics:

Advantages:

- Probiotics are live bacteria and yeast that keep our gut system healthy.
- Probiotics help to replace the lost bacteria during diarrhea and helps in preventing diarrhea. Strains like *Lactobacillus rhamnosus, Saccharomyces boulardii,* and *lactobacillus casei* are associated with reducing the risk of diarrhea.
- It helps in improving mental health conditions.
- Probiotics help in maintaining and reducing LDL, cholesterol and lowers blood pressure.
- Eczema in children and infants may also be reduced by certain strains of probiotics.
- Symptoms of bowel disorders like ulcerative colitis can also be reduced by the help of probiotics.

Disadvantages:

- Rare cases cause bloating, diarrhea, abdominal pain.
- If in excess cause infection that requires medical attention.
- People having on underlying disease or compromised immune system causes potential health problems like skin rash, fever, bloody stools, etc.
- Sometimes interact with immunosuppressive drugs leading to life-threatening conditions. So people taking such drugs should avoid it.

Prebiotics

A prebiotic is a non-viable food component that confers a health benefit on the host associated with modulation of the microbiota.

Amongst colonic foods, it has been shown recently that some components are especially beneficial to health. The components have been called 'prebiotics' defined as a nondigestible food ingredient that beneficially affects the host by selectively stimulating the growth and/or activity of one or a limited number of bacteria in the colon. Prebiotics are thus colonic foods, but they are more than simply malabsorbed, nondigestible or resistant carbohydrates; when they reach the large bowel, they have specific effects that promote the growth of advantageous species of bacteria to the detriment of adverse species.

The microbial flora that lives symbiotically within the large intestine represents an essential element of the physiology of most mammals. The flora thus constitutes a complex ecosystem that needs to be correctly fed in order to maintain a balanced composition in which a healthy promoting bacterial species quantitatively predominant over the potentially harmful species. Foods that resist hydrolysis by the digestive enzymes are not absorbed in the upper part of the gastrointestinal tract, including the small intestine, become a substrate for the colonic microflora. These dietary components pass into the large bowel, where most of the indigenous intestinal microflora are located in a healthy human individual. A wide variety of dietary carbohydrates, especially resistant starch dietary fiber, some polyols, and nondigestible oligosaccharides have such characteristics and they provide quantitatively the majority of colonic food, i.e., dietary components available for bacterial fermentation in the colon. The colonic fermentation of such 'malabsorbed' 'non-digestible' or 'resistant' carbohydrates (oligosaccharides and polysaccharides) play a role in salvaging part of the energy of these dietary components, in controlling transit time, stool bulking , stool frequency, in influencing nutrient, especially mineral ,bioavailability, in producing short-chain fatty acids that are known to play physiological roles such as control of mucosal motility and epithelial cell proliferation, or in modulating immune activity and endocrine functions.

Mode of action of prebiotics

Prebiotics affect intestinal bacteria by increasing the number of beneficial anaerobic bacteria and decreasing the population of potentially pathogenic microorganisms. Probiotics affect the intestinal ecosystem by stimulating mucosal immune mechanisms and by stimulating nonimmune mechanisms through antagonism and competition with potential pathogens. These phenomena are thought to mediate the most beneficial effects, including reduction of the incidence and severity of diarrhea, which is one of the most widely recognized uses for probiotics. Probiotics reduce the risk of colon cancer in animal models, probably due to their role in suppressing the activity of certain bacterial enzymes that may increase the levels of procarcinogens, but this has not been proven in humans.

Functions

- The inclusion of prebiotics in the diet can lead ultimately to a marked change in the composition of the colonic microflora,e.g. By selectively stimulating the growth of bacteria that are generally recognized as being beneficial for health and at the same time, reducing the number of potentially harmful bacteria.

- The most efficient prebiotics identified today stimulate the growth of Bifidobacteria, and sometimes lactobacilli, whilst reducing the numbers and activities of potentially pathogenic organisms.
- The contents of the human gut are not readily accessible for microbiological analysis; therefore a demonstration of changes in the composition of the fecal microflora is often used as a surrogate marker for the prebiotic effect. However, for such a demonstration to be convincing, it is critical that as many components of the fecal microbiota as possible are measured. These should include at least bacteroides, Bifidobacteria, Clostridia, eubacteria, gram-positive cocci, coliforms, Lactobacilli, total aerobes, total anaerobes. Simple stimulation of growth of Bifidobacteria and/or lactobacilli is insufficient to substantiate a prebiotic property without determining the effects on the fecal microorganisms since it is the selectivity of the effect that determines classification as a prebiotic.

Clearly, studies using pure bacterial cultures are of very limited, if any, a value in this respect unless they are supported by mixed culture work in a well-validated set-up. But the ultimate proof must come from human studies in which correctly collected and stored fecal samples are analyzed for their composition in terms of bacterial species that are further well characterized using classical techniques combined with a conventional microbiological approach towards identification and modem molecular genotyping methods. Indeed, it is the effect of the prebiotic in a competitive ecological environment that is important.

Characteristics of Prebiotics

- Should not be hydrolyzed or absorbed in the upper part of G.I tract.
- Should be a selective substrate for one or a limited number of potential bacterial commercials to the colon culture protagonist.
- Should be able to alter the colonic microflora towards a healthier composition or selectively stimulates the growth and or activity of intestinal bacteria associated with health and well-being.
- Should help increase the absorption of certain minerals such as calcium and magnesium.
- Favorable effect on the immune system and provide improved resistance against infection.

References

1. Ohland CL, Macnaughton WK: Probiotic bacteria and intestinal epithelial barrier function. Am J Physiol Gastrointest Liver Physiol 2010; 298:G807–G819.

2. Hooper LV, Wong MH, Thelin A, Hansson L, Falk PG, Gordon JI: Molecular analysis of commensal host-microbial relationships in the intestine. Science 2001; 291: 881–884.

3. Hooper LV, Stappenbeck TS, Hong CV, Gordon JI: Angiogenins: a new class of microbicidal proteins involved in innate immunity. Nat Immunol 2003; 4: 269–273.

4. Sartor RB: Mechanisms of disease: pathogenesis of Crohn's disease and ulcerative colitis. Nat Clin Pract Gastroenterol Hepatol 2006; 3: 390–407.

5. Juntunen M, Kirjavainen PV, Ouwehand AC, Salminen SJ, Isolauri E: Adherence of probiotic bacteria to human intestinal mucus in healthy infants and during rotavirus infection. Clin Diag Lab Immunol 2001; 8: 293–296.

6. Beachey EH: Bacterial adherence: adhesion receptor interactions mediating the attachment of bacteria to mucosal surfaces. J InfectDis 1981; 143: 325–345.

7. Schiffrin EJ, Brassart D, Servin AL, Rochat F, Donnet-Hughes A: Immune modulation of blood leukocytes in humans by lactic acid bacteria: criteria for strain selection. Am J Clin Nutr 1997; 66: 515S–520S.

8. Perdigon G, Maldonado Galdeano C, Valdez JC, Medici M: Interaction of lactic acid bacteria with the gut immune system. Eur J Clin Nutr 2002; 56:S21–S26.

9. Hirano J, Yoshida T, Sugiyama T, Koide N, Mori I, Yokochi T: The effect of *Lactobacillus rhamnosus* on enterohemorrhagic *Escherichia coli* infection of human intestinal cellsin vitro. Microbiol Immunol 2003; 47: 405–409.

10. Salminen S, Bouley C, Boutron-Ruault MC, Cummings JH, Franck A, Gibson GR, Isolauri E, Moreau MC, Roberfroid M, Rowland I: Functional food science and gastrointestinal physiology and function. Br J Nutr 1998; 80:S147–S171.

11. Collado MC, Gueimonde M, Hernández M, Sanz Y, Salminen S: Adhesion of selected *Bifidobacterium* strains to human intestinal mucus and the role of adhesion in enteropathogen exclusion. J Food Prot 2005; 68: 2672–2678.

12. Crociani J, Grill JP, Huppert M, Ballongue J: Adhesion of different bifidobacterias strains to human enterocyte-like Caco-2 cells and comparison with in vivo study. Lett Appl Microbiol 1995; 21: 146–148.

13. Castagliuolo I, Galeazzi F, Ferrari S, Elli M,Brun P, Cavaggioni A, Tormen D, Sturniolo GC, Morelli L, Palù G: Beneficial effect of auto-aggregating Lactobacillus crispatus on experimentally induced colitis in mice. FEMS Immunol Med Microbiol 2005; 43: 197–204.

14. González-Rodríguez I, Sánchez B, Ruiz L,Turroni F, Ventura M, Ruas-Madiedo P,Gueimonde M, Margolles A: Role of extracellular transaldolase from *Bifidobacteriumbifidum* in mucin adhesion and aggregation. Appl Environ Microbiol 2012; 78: 3992–3998.

15. Neutra MR, Forstner JF: Gastrointestinal mucus: synthesis, secretion and function; in Johnson LR (ed): Physiology of the Gastrointestinal Tract, ed 2. New York, Raven, 1987.

16. Ouwehand AC, Salminen S, Tolkko S, Roberts P, Ovaska J, Salminen E: Resected human colonic tissue: new model for characterizing adhesion of lactic acid bacteria. Clin Diag Lab Immunol 2002; 9: 184–186.

17. Haller D, Colbus H, Ganzle MG, Scherenbacher P, Bode C, Hammes WP: Metabolic and functional properties of lactic acid bacteria in the gastro-intestinal ecosystem: a comparative in vitro study between bacteria of intestinal and fermented food origin. SystAppl Microbiol 2001; 24: 218–226.

18. Van Tassell ML, Miller MJ: Lactobacillus adhesion to mucus. Nutrients 2011; 3: 613–636.

19. Buck BL, Altermann E, Svingerud T, Klaen-hammer TR: Functional analysis of putativeadhesion factors in Lactobacillus acidophilus NCNCFM. Appl Environ Microbiol 2005; 71: 8344–8351.

20. Vélez MP, De Keersmaecker SC, Vanderleyden J: Adherence factors of Lactobacillus in the human gastrointestinal tract. FEMS Microbiol Lett 2007; 276: 140–148.

21. Gómez-Llorente C, Muñoz S, Gil A: Role of Toll-like receptors in the development of immunotolerance mediated by probiotics. Proc Nutr Soc 2010; 69: 381–389.

22. Lebeer S, Vanderleyden J, De Keersmaecker CJ: Host interactions of probiotic bacterial surface molecules: comparison with commensals and pathogens. Nat Rev Microbiol 2010; 8: 171–184.

23.https://www.ncbi.nlm.nih.gov/pmc/articles/PMC5390821/#idm139886653943952title

24.https://www.sciencedirect.com/topics/agricultural-and-biological-sciences/prebiotics

Chapter-4

MICROMINERAL: SELENIUM

Nidhi Joshi

Ph.D. Scholar, Dept. Food and Nutrition, College of Home Science, G.B.P.U.A. & T., Pantnagar, U.S. Nagar, Uttarakhand- 263145

Phone no. +919535950495
Email: nidhicuty.80@gmail.com

ABSTRACT

Selenium is an essential trace mineral necessary for cellular functions. Whole grain cereals, wheat, sunflower seeds, brazil nuts, eggs, organ meats, garlic, mushrooms, and seafood are the important food sources of selenium. Selenium compounds are very efficiently absorbed by humans. In the body, selenium can be bound to selenium-binding proteins. Selenium plays an important role in three major enzymes system i.e., glutathione peroxidase, thioredoxin reductase, iodothyronine deiodinases. Selenium possesses antioxidant properties and protects from free radical damage. Selenium regulates iodine metabolism and modulates immune function. An ecological deficiency of selenium has been observed which leads to cardiomyopathy, osteoarthropathy, hypothyroidism and increased susceptibility to infection. Excess of selenium results in selenosis. Thus, the present chapter deals with advanced details about the micromineral selenium.

Keywords - Selenium, Glutathione peroxidase, Keshan disease, Kashchin-Beck disease, Selenosis

Introduction

Selenium is one of the "newer" minerals discovered during the 20th century as being both required and toxic with a relatively narrow range of intake between the two. The existence of selenium as the metal was first reported by J. J. Berzelius in 1817. In 1957, selenium was recognized as an essential nutrient for normal growth and reproduction in animals. Selenium was identified as an integral part of the selenoenzyme cytoplasmic glutathione peroxidase (GSHpx) in 1973.

Selenium is a non-metallic element and exists in several oxidation states which include Se^{2+}, Se^{4+} and Se^{6+}. Selenium appears black and shiny. If ground it appears black but if ground extremely fine it appears red. Its molecular weight is 78.96 and its atomic weight is 34. The chemistry of selenium is similar to that of sulfur. Selenium replaces sulfur to form organic compounds such as selenocysteine and selenomethionine. The total selenium content of the body varies from 3-15 mg depending on the dietary intake. Approximately 30% of tissue selenium is contained in the liver, 15% in the kidney, 30% in muscles and 10% in blood plasma.

Food Sources

Much of the variation in the Se content of foods and feeds is due to large scale geographical differences in environmental Se. Environmental conditions and agricultural practices have a profound influence on the selenium content of many foods. Table 1 illustrates the wide range of selenium content of the principal food groups and the variability in the selenium content of dietary constituents in selected countries.

Table1: Typical ranges of selenium concentrations (ng/g fresh weight) in food groups

Food group	India	United States	International compilation
Cereals and cereal product	5-95	10-370	10-550
Meat, meat products, and eggs	40-120	100-810	10-360
Fish and marine	280-1080	400-1500	110-970
Fish and freshwater	-	-	180-680
Pulses	10-138	-	-
Dairy products	5-15	10-130	1-170
Fruits and vegetables	1-7	1-60	1-20

Source: Vitamin and mineral requirement in Human Nutrition, FAO/WHO (2004)

Selenium enters the food chain through plants. The concentration of selenium in plants is directly related to the concentration of the mineral in soil on which plants were grown. The Se contents of foods of animal origin depend on large part on the Se intakes of livestock.

The most important sources of Se are whole grain cereals, wheat, sunflower seeds, brazil nuts, eggs, organ meats, garlic, mushrooms, and seafood. Selenium occurs in foods in organic forms, such as selenomethionine, selenocysteine, selenocysteine, and Se-methyl selenomethionine. In general, plant foods contain a greater proportion of organic selenium compounds. Inorganic forms include selenite (H_2SO_3) and selenate (H_2SO_4). These forms are found in some vegetables.

Metabolism

Selenium compounds are generally very efficiently absorbed by humans and selenium absorption does not appear to be under homeostatic control. Selenium is mainly absorbed from the duodenum. Almost 50-80% of dietary selenium is absorbed, with efficiency being higher for organic forms, as compared to inorganic. Among organic forms, selenomethionine is better absorbed than selenocysteine. Among inorganic forms, selenates are better absorbed than selenites. In addition, some dietary factors appear to influence the absorption of the element. Phytates and heavy metals, such as mercury through chelation and precipitation, hinder selenium absorption. Vitamin C, A, and E, as well as glutathione, enhance the absorption.

After absorption selenium binds to sulfhydryl groups in α and β globulins of VLDL and LDL to be transported to the different tissues. Liver and kidneys appear to be the major target organs. Inorganic forms of selenium are passively transported whereas organic forms are actively transported.

Within tissues such as liver, organic, as well as, inorganic selenium compounds have different fates. This is briefly discussed herewith:

1. *Selenomethionine* obtained from the diet may be:
   - stored as such in the amino acid pool,
   - used for protein synthesis, and
   - catabolized to selenocysteine.
2. *Selenocysteine* obtained from the diet or after catabolism of selenomethionine is degraded to yield free elemental selenium. This elemental selenium may be:
   - attached to tRNA charged with serine to be incorporated in selenium-dependent enzymes, and
   - converted into selenite which may be stored or excreted.
3. *Selenate* from the diet is converted to *selenite*. Selenite is further converted to *selenide*. Selenide may be:
   - converted to selenophosphate to yield free selenium, which is incorporated into enzymes, and
   - excreted as methyl selenide.
4. Selenium is excreted from the body almost equally in the urine (as methyl selenium) and feces (unabsorbed selenium, biliary, pancreatic and intestinal secretion). Selenium losses through lungs and skin also contribute to daily selenium excretion.

Selenoprotein

In the body, selenium can be bound to selenium-binding proteins. It can also be directly incorporated into selenoprotein during translation at the ribosome complex using an RNA specific for the amino acid- *selenocysteine*. Thus, selenocysteine can be considered as the 21st amino acid in terms of ribosome-mediated protein synthesis. At least 15 selenoproteins have now been characterized. Table 2 provides a list of these selenoproteins.

Table 2: A selection of characterized selenoproteins

Protein	Tissue distribution
Cytosolic GSHPx	All, including thyroid
Phospholipid hydroperoxide GSHPx	All, including thyroid
Gastrointestinal GSHPx	Gastrointestinal tract
Extracellular GSHPx	Plasma, thyroid
Thioredoxin reductase (Trx-red)	All, including thyroid
Iodothyronine- deiodinase (type 1) (DIO 1)	Liver, kidneys, and thyroid
Iodothyronine- deiodinase (type 2) (DIO 2)	The central nervous system, and pituitary
Iodothyronine- deiodinase (type 3) (DIO 3)	Brown adipose tissue, central nervous system, and placenta
Selenoprotein P	Plasma
Selenoprotein W	Muscle
Sperm capsule selenoprotein	Sperm tail

*GSHPx, glutathione peroxidase

Functions

Selenium is a component of glutathione peroxidase which along with vitamin E and superoxide dismutase forms a part of the antioxidant defense system. Selenoproteins in animals and humans are involved in protection from oxidative damage, maintaining adequate thyroid hormone status and protection from injury by a heavy metal like mercury.

Three major enzyme systems in which selenium plays an important role have been identified in humans. These include:

    a. Glutathione peroxidases,
    b. Thioredoxin reductase
    c. Iodothyronine deiodinases, and
    d. Selenoprotein P and W

Glutathione Peroxidases

A. *Cellular Oxidant protection*

The role of selenium in the cytosolic enzyme, glutathione peroxidase (GSHpx), was first illustrated in 1973. Four selenium-dependent glutathione peroxidases have been identified and named as Glutathione peroxidases 1-4 ($GSHP_{XS}$ 1-4). During stress, infection, or tissue injury, selenoenzyme may protect against damaging effects of hydrogen peroxide or oxygen-rich free radicals. This family of enzymes catalyzes the destruction of hydrogen peroxide or lipid hydroperoxides according to the following general reactions:

$$H_2O_2 + 2GSH \qquad 2H_2O + GSSG \longrightarrow$$

$$ROOH + 2GSH \qquad ROH + H_2O + GSSG$$

where GSH is glutathione and GSSG is its oxidized form.

Thus, from the reaction above, it is evident that the main role of glutathione peroxidases is to reduce hydrogen peroxide and free hydroperoxides in different cells and tissues by using glutathione (GSH) as the hydrogen donor. Thus, the reactive species of hydroperoxides free radicals are converted into innocuous molecules of water. $GSHP_{x-1}$ is present in virtually all cells, $GSHP_{x-2}$ is localized in the gastrointestinal tract, $GSHP_{x-3}$ is present in plasma while $GSHP_{x-4}$ is most abundant in testis but present in other tissues also.

B. *Prostaglandin Metabolism*

SeGSHpx is found in very high concentration in platelets and its function there involves the reduction of lipid peroxides. The metabolic pathway of arachidonic acid is presented in Figure 1.

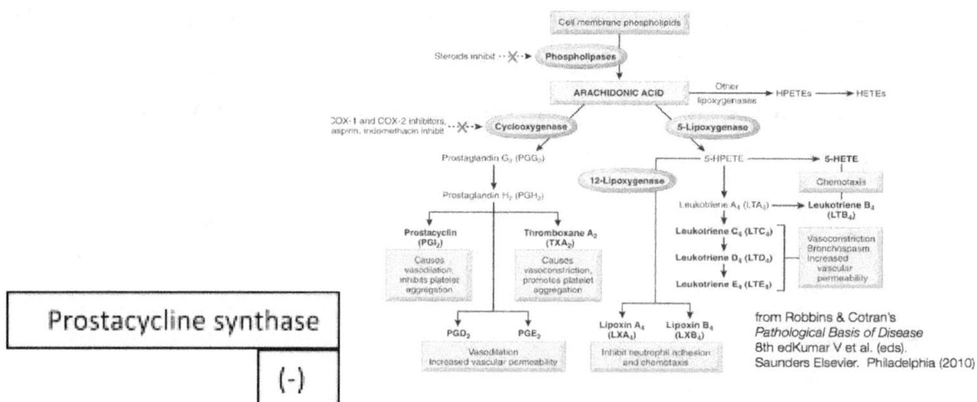

Fig. 1: Metabolic pathway of arachidonic acid

SeGSHPx catalyzes the conversion of L-12-hydroperoxy-5,8,11,14-eicosatetraenoic acid (12-HPETE) to hydro-5,8,11,14-eicosatetraenoic acid (HETE). HPETE and other hydroxyl acids inhibit prostacyclin synthase. Therefore, if SeGSHPx activity were low, as in Se deficiency, the resulting accumulation of HPETE would result in an imbalance of prostacyclin and thromboxanes, leading to increased platelet aggregation and vasoconstriction.

Thioredoxin Reductase
The selenoenzyme thioredoxin reductase is involved in the disposal of the products of oxidative metabolism. It contains two selenocysteine groups per molecule and is a major component of a redox system with a multiplicity of functions. Thioredoxin reductase reduces oxidized thioredoxin in the presence of NADPH. Reduced thioredoxin serves as an electron donor for thioredoxin peroxidase which consequently reduces H_2O_2 to H_2O. Reduced thioredoxin provides reducing equivalents for various redox-dependent systems, such as ribonucleotide reductase essential for DNA synthesis, redox regulation of transcription factors. Besides, these proteins have important functions in regulating cell growth and inhibiting apoptosis.

Iodothyronine Deiodinases
Selenoprotein, iodothyronine deiodinases (DIO) essential for the conversion of thyroxine or tetraiodothyronine (T_4) to its physiologically active form triiodothyronine (T_3). Three types of iodothyronine deiodinases have been identified, all of them being selenoproteins. *Type I iodothyronine deiodinases*are found in the liver, kidney and thyroid tissues. The major role of this enzyme is to provide T_3 to peripheral tissues by deiodination T_4 secreted by the thyroid gland. *Type II iodothyronine deiodinases* are present in the brain, pituitary, and placenta. The major function of this enzyme is to regulate T_3 levels in these tissues and control the secretion of thyroid-stimulating hormone. *Type III iodothyronine deiodinases* are involved mainly in the degradation of the T_3 and T_4.

Selenoprotein P & W
Selenoprotein P, an extracellular constituent with multiple selenocysteine molecules. Se-P serves as a Se-transport protein and has an antioxidant role, deactivating free radicals. Selenoprotein W, present in the muscle has a suggested role in muscular degeneration seen in combined selenium and vitamin E deficiency. One of the selenoproteins is a component of the mitochondrial capsule of sperm cells, damage to which leads to sperm abnormality in selenium deficiency.

Selenium & Immune Function

Selenium modulates immune function. Adequate intake of selenium is essential for both cell-mediated and humoral immunity as well as the innate immune response. Selenium increases chemotaxis, phagocytosis as well as bacterial parasite killing by neutrophils and macrophages. Selenium stimulates lymphocytes and NK cells (natural killers). It increases the expression of IL-2 receptors on the cell surface of B and T lymphocytes, thus increasing the ability of these cells to be stimulated by cytokines such as IL-2 (interleukin). It increases B-lymphocytes numbers and their antibody secretion, Th cells, CD4+ cell numbers and their response to mitogens (a substance that induces and stimulates mitosis). It also improves delayed-type hypersensitivity responses and CD8+ T cells show increased cytotoxic action against virus-infected cells when selenium is supplemented.

Selenium Cancer

Several ecological correlational and cross-sectional case-control studies have elucidated that low Se status may increase the risk of cancer in several populations. Epidemiologists have linked a lower selenium intake statistically with a higher incidence of cancer of tongue, breast, lungs, esophagus, stomach, colon, rectum, prostate, ovary, cervix, bladder, pancreas, peritoneum and liver.

Deficiency

Selenium deficiency can develop in premature infants and in persons sustained for long periods of time by selenium-free enteral or parenteral solutions. Symptoms characteristics of deficiency in humans include a decline in glutathione peroxidase activity in a variety of cell types, fragile red blood cells, enlarged heart, cardiomyopathy, growth retardation, cataract formation, abnormal placenta retention, deficient spermatogenesis, and skeletal muscle degeneration.

Keshan Disease

Keshan disease is a selenium responsive cardiomyopathy that mainly affects children and women in child-bearing age in certain areas of China. This develops in children whose intakes are less than 17µg/d. The disease was first studied with respect to its epidemiology, clinical signs, and pathology on the occasion of an outbreak in Keshan County, Heilongjiang Province, China, in 1935.

Etiology

Affected areas are low in soil Se (i.e., topsoils containing less than 125 ppb Se, of which less than 3 ppb is water-soluble), thereby producing plant foods and feeds of low Se content (e.g., food and feed grains in affected areas generally contain less than 40 ppb Se). Coxsackievirus is mainly non-virulent and Se deficiency it becomes virulent and pathogenic and further increases expression of cardiac lesion of Keshan disease.

Typical manifestations are fatigue after even mild exercise, cardiac arrhythmia and palpitations, loss of appetite, cardiac insufficiency, cardiomegaly, and congestive heart failure. Pathological changes include multifocal necrosis and fibrosis.

Subtype of Keshan disease

Four clinical subtypes of Keshan disease have been identified (Table 3).

Table 3: Subtyping of Keshan disease

Acute type	Chronic type	Subacute type	Latent type
Acute heart function insufficiency: • Cardiogenic shock • Heart-brain syndrome • Pulmonary edema • Severe arrhythmia	Moderate or severe cardiac enlargement, usually with congestive heart failure	Moderately rapid onset; usually with signs and symptoms of both acute and chronic types Most prevalent in children	Mild cardiac enlargement without abnormal heart function
Symptoms: • Dizziness • Malaise • Loss of appetite • Nausea • Vomiting • Chills • Dyspnea	**Symptoms:** • Palpitation • Consciousness of heartbeat at rest • Shortness of breath • Edema • Oliguria • Cough with hemoptysis • Right upper quadrant pain	**Symptoms:** • Malaise • Restlessness • Facial edema • Gallop rhythm • Cardiac dilation	**Symptoms:** • Dizziness • Fatigue • Palpitation after exercise

Treatment

Several intervention studies have demonstrated that Se can be very effective in the prevention of this disease. Selenium supplementation was found to reduce the severity of disease manifestations. But selenium supplements cannot reverse cardiac failure if it has occurred.

Kaschin-beck Disease

Kaschin-Beck disease is an endemic osteoarthropathy (bone and joint disease) that has linked with low selenium status. The disease primarily affects children between the ages of 5 and 13 years living in certain regions of China, eastern Siberia, northern Korea. It is characterized by osteoarthritis involving degeneration and necrosis of the joints and epiphyseal- plate cartilages of legs and arms. Long bones are most frequently affected. The most striking histological feature of Kaschin-Beck disease is Chondronecrosis with the proliferation of surviving chondrocytes in clusters. The condition results in enlarged joints (especially of the fingers, toes, and knees), shortened fingers, toes and extremities, and, in severe cases, dwarfism. Kaschin-Beck disease occurs in areas where the availability of soil selenium for crop growth is low. The selenium content of hair and of whole blood are abnormally low and the blood content of GSHPx is reduced.

Treatment

Se tablets were effective in reducing the severity and in facilitating the improvement of the disease. Supplementation of Se is effective in reducing the incidence of disease.

Selenium And Thyroid Hormone

Selenium deficiency causes a decline in activity of type I and type II iodothyronine deiodinases. Combined deficiency of selenium and iodine produces much more severe hypothyroidism compared to iodine deficiency alone. Further, maternal deficiency of selenium and iodine is implicated in cretinism in newborns.

Selenium Status And Susceptibility To Infection

Suboptimal selenium status affects immune-competence with the impairment of both cell-mediated immunity and β-cell function. The early preclinical stages of development of HIV infection are accompanied by a very marked decline in plasma selenium. The virulence of RNA virus such as hepatitis B was enhanced by a decline in selenium status.

Toxicity

Toxicity of selenium in the body leads to selenosis. There is a narrow margin between the beneficial and harmful intakes of selenium.Selenosis occurs when the intake of selenium is more than 850-900 µg per day. Symptoms of chronic toxicity include brittle hair and nails, skin lesions with secondary infections and garlic odor in the breath. Chronic selenium poisoning in people is characterized primarily by loss of hair and changes in fingernail morphology.

ASSESSMENT OF SELENIUM STATUS

Glutathione peroxidase activity has been used as an index of selenium status in humans. Several different human tissues, including blood, plasma, hair, and toenails, have been analyzed for their selenium content as a way of assessing nutritional selenium status.

REQUIREMENTS

The FAO/WHO 2004 recommendations for nutrient intake for selenium by groups is given in Table 4.

Table 4: Recommended Nutrient Intake of Selenium, by group

Group	Assumed weight (kg)	RNI (µg/day)
Infants and children		
0-6 months	6	6
7-12 months	9	10
1-3 years	12	17
4-6 years	19	22
7-9 years	25	21
Adolescents		
Females, 10-18 years	49	26
Males, 10-18 years	51	32
Adults		
Females, 19-65 years	55	26
65+ years	54	25
Males, 19-65 years	65	34
65+ years	64	33
Pregnant women, 2nd trimester	-	28
3rd trimester	-	30
Lactating women, 0-6 months	-	35
7-12 months	-	42

Source: Vitamin and mineral requirements in Human Nutrition, FAO/WHO (2004)

SITUATION IN INDIA

There have been few studies on Se nutrition in the Indian population. Most of the available information is from NIN. Se deficiency or depletion does not appear to be a problem and the dietary intake (71-163 µg/day) is consistent with the RDA of 36 and 26 µg (for males and females, respectively) as suggested by FAO/WHO. A level of 40 µg/day can be recommended as the acceptable intake of Se for Indians.

REFERENCES

1. *Advanced Nutrition* (2006)Indira Gandhi National Open University, New Delhi, p 323-330.

2. Berdanier CD and Zempleni J (2009) Advanced Nutrition: Macronutrients, Micronutrients and Metabolism. 2ⁿᵈedn, CRC Press Taylor & Francis Group, New York, p 411-415.

3. Combs GF and Combs SB (1986)The role of selenium in nutrition. Academic Press Inc., London.

4. Joint FAO/WHO (2004)Vitamin and mineral requirement in Human Nutrition. A report of the joint FAO/WHO expert consultation, Bangkok, Thailand, 21-30 September 1998, 2ⁿᵈedn, p 194-211.

5. Indian Council of Medical Research (ICMR) *Nutrients Requirements and Recommended Dietary Allowances for Indians.* A Report of the Expert Group of Indian Council of Medical Research (2010), National Institute of Nutrition, Hyderabad.

6. Shetty PS (2010)Nutrition, immunity, and infection. Cambridge University Press, Cambridge, UK, p 37-38.

7. *Trace elements in human nutrition and health* (1996) A report prepared in collaboration with the FAO/IAEA. p 105-120. World Health Organization (WHO), Geneva, Switzerland.

Chapter-5

PRECISION NUTRIENT MANAGEMENT FOR ENHANCING QUALITY OF SOLANACEOUS CROPS: AN ECONOMIC ANALYSIS

Sourav Ghosh

PhD Research Scholar, Indian Agricultural Research Institute, Pusa,
New Delhi, Pin-110012, India

and

Debarati Datta

PhD Research Scholar, Govind Ballabh Pant University of Agriculture and Technology,
Pantnagar, Distt- Udham Singh Nagar, Uttarakhand, Pin-263145, India

ABSTRACT

'Precision Farming' or 'Precision Agriculture' aims at increasing productivity, production and minimizing the environmental impact of farming. Brinjal, tomato, and potato are important vegetable crops in India. India ranks 2nd, 3rd and 2nd in area, 2nd, 2nd and 3rd in production and 8th, 10th and 4th in productivity for brinjal, tomato and potato respectively. A number of crop-specific precision technologies have been developed for Indian farmers like drip irrigation, grid soil sampling, yield map based fertilizer recommendations, site-specific management, etc. In this context, the objective of this paper is to analyze the production and productivity pattern of tomato, brinjal, and potato under precision and conventional farming systems. Specifically, this paper has looked into the production, productivity, income and yield gap analysis of the above crops. Policy suggestions for the government have been provided. A number of papers have been critically reviewed and consolidated points have been discussed in this paper in the subsequent sections. The percent increase in gross returns for brinjal, tomato, and potato under precision farming was found to be 51.3 percent, 120.2 percent and 80.5 percent over non-precision method while the percent yield increase was 34.0 percent, 80.2 percent, and 52.0 percent respectively. This paper is expected to help the adoption of precision farming in horticultural crops and also aid in future research.

Keywords: Precision agriculture, solanaceous vegetables, economic analysis, technology adoption, policy suggestions

1. Introduction

The growth in agriculture over a period of time has remained lower than the growth in the non-agriculture sector and this decelerating trend is a cause of concern. The gap between growth in agriculture and non-agriculture sectors began to widen in 1981-82, and more particularly, since 1996-97, because of acceleration in the growth of industry and services sectors (Agropedia, 2012). Notably, the agricultural growth performance could not be sustained during the 1990s because of decelerations in yield and output growth rates in both food and non-food crops. A comparison of decadal growth in the area, production, and productivity of food grains since the 1950s reveals that India has been experiencing stagnation or negative growth in these crops.

Increasing agricultural productivity perhaps remains the single most important determinant of economic growth and poverty reduction, and hence provides the key to the millennium development goal. Improvements in productivity come from adoption of new technologies and increase in production efficiency. 'Precision farming' or 'Precision Agriculture' aims at increasing productivity, decreasing production costs and minimizing the environmental impact of farming (Mondal *et al*, 2007). The management of in-field variability in soil fertility and crop conditions for improving crop production and minimizing the environmental impact is the crux of precision farming. New technologies, such as Global Positioning Systems (GPS), sensors, satellites or aerial images, and Geographical Information Systems (GIS) are utilized to assess and analyze variations in agricultural production.

Vegetables being short duration and high-value cash crops have high scope for implementation of precision agriculture (PA) technologies. Moreover, there are excellent export opportunities for vegetables. Vegetables grown with simple PA technologies like drip irrigation, site-specific input management, soil map based fertilizer application have been found to be superior to those grown under conventional techniques- both in yield and quality, with much higher Benefit-Cost ratio (Shibusawa, 2002). Moreover, the PA farms have been found to be more ecologically sustainable and environmentally friendly with reduced chemical inputs and water wastage, hence causing less pollution. The problems like soil salinity due to excessive fertilizer application, leaching of nutrients to groundwater, eutrophication of water bodies, etc. can be significantly reduced through precision agriculture.

The main problem of implementation of this new technology is the high initial set-up cost which a majority of Indian farmers are unable to afford. Even those farmers who can afford are not sure of the benefits leading to rather a slow adoption of this technology in India (Pinaki *et al.*, 2011).

Keeping these points in view, the objectives set were;
i.   To make an economic analysis of a precision agriculture farm and compare with conventional farm with special reference to three solanaceous vegetables viz. tomato, brinjal, and potato.
ii.   To study the main constraints in the adoption of precision agriculture technology in the country.
iii.   To suggest government policies that can lead to greater adoption of this technology in India.

2. Precision Agriculture Technology Available For Vegetables

2.1 Hard PA technologies
Hard PA technologies include a vast array of tools of hardware, software and equipment. These are:

1. **Global Positioning System (GPS) receivers:** GPS provides continuous position information in real-time, while in motion. Having precise location information at any time allows soil and crop measurements to be mapped.

2. **Differential Global Positioning System (DGPS):** A technique to improve GPS accuracy that uses pseudo-range errors measured at a known location to improve the measurements made by other GPS receivers.

3. **Geographic information systems (GIS):** Store layers of information, such as yields, yield maps, soil survey maps, remotely sensed data, crop scouting reports, and soil nutrient levels. They are used in generating maps.

4. **Remote sensing (RS):** It is the collection of data from a distance. Remotely-sensed data provide a tool for evaluating crop health. Plant stress related to moisture, nutrients, compaction, crop diseases and other plant health concerns is often easily detected in overhead images. Remote sensing can reveal in-season variability that affects crop yield and can be time enough to make management decisions that improve profitability for the current crop.

5. **Variable Rate Applicator (VRA):** Includes equipment like automatic fertilizer applicator which can adjust the inputs according to the nutrient map loaded to the system.

2.2 Soft PA technologies

These are simple low-cost technologies developed specifically for developing countries. These include:

1. **Drip irrigation system**- Precise and regulated application of irrigation water and plant nutrients at low pressure and frequent intervals through drippers/emitters directly into the root zone of the plant with the help of a close network of pipes is known as drip irrigation system.

2. **Chlorophyll meter (SPAD) and Leaf Color Chart (LCC)** – for measurement of the crop N status in rice fields to determine the timing of N top dressing.

3. **Site-Specific Nutrient Management (SSNM)** based on manual soil testing.

4. **Community nurseries** – equipped with modern facilities.

2.3 Precision technologies developed in Tomato, Brinjal and Potato in India

The common precision farming technologies used in Tomato and Brinjal include raising seedling in community-based nursery, site-specific nutrient management, SPAD and LCC based nitrogen application , building of soil nutrient maps through remote sensing (RS), precise application of chemicals for plant protection, drip irrigation and combine harvesters (Srinivasan *et al.*, 2006) .

Potato is highly responsive to nitrogenous fertilizer. Sufficient nitrogen content in plant tissues needs to be maintained throughout the crop growth period to optimize potato tuber yield. Chlorophyll content in leaves is directly correlated with nitrogen. However, monitoring nitrogen supply in the plant tissues through field sampling, extraction and chemical analysis of either N or chlorophyll is time-consuming and costly. A non-destructive rapid field measuring instrument SPAD (Soil Plant Analysis Development) 502 for leaf greenness or relative chlorophyll content has been developed by MINOLTA. This instrument was found to be a promising tool to assess N status of potato foliage which has been found to increase the tuber yield of potato by almost 22 percent.

3. Economic Analysis Of Precision Agriculture In Solanaceous Crops – Tomato, Brinjal, And Potato

3.1 Methodology

A study was conducted in the Dharmapuri district and data on precision and non-precision farmings were collected through the interview schedule. The respondents were selected randomly from the five identified blocks in such a way that there were 35 adopters and 35 nonadopters of precision farming in each tomato, brinjal and potato crops, making the total sample to be of 210 respondents. Differences in productivity, income, and employment under the precision and conventional farmings were worked out from the cost cultivation data (Maheswari *et al.*, 2012).

3.2 Results And Discussion

Economics of tomato production were estimated for precision and non-precision methods of cultivation and the results are presented in Table 1.

From the table, it can be seen that the share in total variable cost in the case of precision farmers was highest for fertilizer (27.15%), followed by human labor (25.04%). Within the cost of human labor, 72.21 percent was paid out to hired labor and the rest was imputed value of family labor. In non-precision farming, plant protection chemical was found to be the major input, accounting for 31.06 percent of the total cost, followed by human labor (25.47%), fertilizer (9.70%) and seedlings (7.90%). The gross margin calculated as the difference between the gross return and variable cost was 166 percent higher in precision than non-precision farming in tomato cultivation.

Table 1: Cost of cultivation of tomato

Sl No.	Particulars	Precision farming (Rs/ha)	Non-precision farming (Rs/ha)	Difference (%)
1	Human labor	25,693	18382	39.77
2	Machine power	6000	5250	14.28
3	Seedlings	5100	5700	-10.52
4	Manures	7292	4000	82.3
5	Plant protection chemicals	9410	22420	-58.02
6	Fertilizers	27858	7004	297.73
7	Stacking	5666	4700	20.56
8	Drip system	8850	0	100
9	Interest on working capital @ 7 %	6710	4721	42.15
10	Total variable cost	102581	72178	42.15

11	Main product (kg/ha)	78663	43662	80.16
12	Gross returns	432649	196480	120.2
13	Gross margin	330068	124302	165.54

Economics of brinjal production was estimated for precision and non-precision methods of cultivation and the results are presented in Table 2.

Labor cost accounted for the highest share in total variable cost in precision farming and it was 49.57 percent more than that of non-precision farming. The cost of fertilizer was the second-highest, with 151.66 percent more in precision farming, mainly due to the high cost of water-soluble fertilizers. Non-precision farmers spent 123.64 percent higher cost on plant protection chemicals because of the high use of these chemicals. The spending on seedlings, machine power, and manures was more are less the same in both cases. The precision farmers incurred a total cost of Rs 1,10,900/ ha, which was 25.47 percent higher than by non-precision farmers, but realized 77.61 percent higher net return over non-precision farmers. The gross margin calculated as the difference between the gross return and variable cost was 67 percent higher in precision than non-precision farming in brinjal cultivation.

Table 2: Cost of cultivation of brinjal

Sl No.	Particulars	Precision farming (Rs/ha)	Non-precision farming (Rs/ha)	Difference (%)
1	Human labor	38,668	25853	49.57
2	Machine power	6000	5340	12
3	Seedlings	4800	5100	-6.25
4	Manures	6031	5975	0.93
5	Plant protection chemicals	13441	30061	-123.64
6	Fertilizers	25853	10273	151.66
7	Drip system	8850	0	100
8	Interest on working capital @ 7 %	7685	5782	32.92
9	Total variable cost	110900	88386	25.47
10	Main product (kg/ha)	77626	55928	34

| 11 | Gross returns | 350633 | 231714 | 51.32 |
| 12 | Gross margin | 239733 | 1143327 | 67.26 |

Economics of potato production was estimated for precision and non-precision methods of cultivation and the results are presented in Table 3.

Fertilizer cost accounted for the highest share in total variable cost in precision farming and it was 88.45 percent more than that of non-precision farming. The cost of machine power was the second-highest, with 83.3 percent more in precision farming. Non-precision farmers spent 40.53 percent higher cost on plant protection chemicals because of the high use of these chemicals. The spendings on human labor and manures were more are less the same in both cases. The precision farmers incurred a total cost of Rs 1,21,039/ ha, which was 28.42 percent higher than by non-precision farmers, but realized 80.50 percent higher net return over non-precision farmers. The gross margin calculated as the difference between the gross return and variable cost was 152.94 percent higher in precision than non-precision farming in potato cultivation.

Table 3: Cost of cultivation of Potato

Sl No.	Particulars	Precision farming (Rs/ha)	Non-precision farming (Rs/ha)	Difference (%)
1	Human labor	26,325	21818.5	20.65
2	Machine power	10500	5727.27	83.33
3	Seeds	25,500	31363.63	-18.69
4	Manures	6245.5	5454.54	14.50
5	Plant protection chemicals	1500	2522.7	-40.53
6	Fertilizers	34050	18068.18	88.45
7	Canal irrigation	0	2727.27	-100
8	Drip system	9000	0	100
9	Interest on working capital @ 7 %	7,918	6567.35	20.57
10	Total variable cost	121,039	94249.44	28.42
11	Main product (kg/ha)	37309.78	24545.45	52.00
12	Gross returns	292409.81	161999.9	80.50

| 13 | Gross margin | 171,371 | 67750.46 | 152.94 |

4. Constraints In Adoption Of Precision Farming In Vegetables

Reasons for non-adoption of precision farming as ranked by the farmers were analyzed through Garrett's ranking technique and the results are presented in Table 4.

The results showed that the lack of finance and credit facilities were the most important reasons for the non-adoption of precision farming. Obtaining credit was a difficult process because farmers could not produce collateral security. Drip installation and use of water-soluble fertilizers were very expensive and required credit. Because of output price fluctuations, farmers were not ready to make investments. Lack of knowledge about precision farming technologies was another important constraint because a majority of small farmers were illiterate and were not able to follow and adopt the latest technologies. Labor scarcity was also a problem in adopting precision farming. Due to urbanization and migration, there was a scarcity of labor for agricultural operations. Since precision farming was highly labor-intensive technology and operations were time-bound, farmers faced the dearth of labor, especially during stacking and harvesting. The traditional farmers had a wrong perception of the higher yield from the précised quantity of inputs. It was a major constraint to the adoption of precision farming. It was found that besides adequate quantum of water for the entire crop duration, and pumping efficiency of the motor should also be about 12000 liters of water per hour, with 1.5 kg pressure for fertigation in precision farming. Lack of water availability and pump efficiency, lack of technical skill, inadequate size of landholding, mindset, and traditional beliefs were constraints to the adoption of precision farming. The local market was not big enough to market the huge quantity of output produced through precision farming, so farmers had to negotiate with supermarkets, etc., but sometimes it led to low prices and less profit.

Table 4: Constraints to adoption of precision farming

Reasons	Mean Garrett's score	Rank
Lack of finance and credit facilities	73	1
Drip installation and water-soluble fertilizers are expensive	65	2
Lack of knowledge about precision farming technologies	54	3
Labour scarcity	53	4
Farmers' perception on yield impact of low quantity of inputs	51	5

Lack of water availability and pumping efficiency	44	6
Lack of technical skill to follow precision farming recommendations	42	7
Market tie-ups lead to low price fixation for the produce / unprofitable negotiations	41	8
Inadequate training and demonstrations and weak research – extension – farmer relationship	41	9
Inadequate size of landholdings for adoption of precision farming	27	10

5. Policy Suggestions For Government

i. Government should create PA societies who will be responsible for technology dissemination to the farmers. These societies should be equipped with required PA equipment, cold storage etc. Moreover buy-back facilities should be available to the farmers which will encourage them to use the PA technologies.

ii. Marketing channels should be strengthened for products developed through PA farms in urban and semi-urban areas.

iii. A direct linkage between producers and supermarkets should be created through these societies which will ease the marketing process.

iv. 'Virtual land consolidation' while keeping ownership structure intact can be a solution of land fragmentation problem of India and can create new roads for PA.

v. Collective farming on a co-operative basis will ease PA implementation.

vi. Nature of crop and weed vary from zone to zone, country to country. So the development of software and hardware for crop and weeds of India, site-specific tillage technique, etc. should be started and these packages will be used for PA.

vii. Nutrient maps along with easy to understand fertilizer recommendation for each management zone within the field can be distributed through 'Panchayats' (Village regulatory body).

viii. Providing subsidies for water-soluble fertilizers and pump-sets will increase the adoption of precision farming.

ix. States, like Punjab, Haryana, have experienced a large scale mechanization as well as high doses of fertilizer and pesticides are more or less suitable for 'hard' PA.

6. Conclusions

The study has revealed that drip irrigation, Leaf Colour Charts (LCC) and SPAD meter based nitrogen application to crops and Site-Specific Nutrients Management (SSNM)are the most commonly followed precision agriculture technologies in solanaceous vegetables viz. tomato, brinjal, and potato. Adoption of precision farming leads to about 80 percent increase in yield in tomato, 34 percent in brinjal and 52 % in potato. An increase in gross margin has been found 165 percent, 67 percent, and 152 percent in tomato, brinjal and potato production, respectively. Lack of finance and credit facilities have been identified as the major constraints for the non-adoption of precision farming. The study has suggested that the development of PA societies, strengthening of marketing channels and providing subsidies on water-soluble fertilizers and pump sets of drip irrigation will increase the adoption of precision farming in India.

References

1. Agropedia. Some successful examples of private sector initiative in Uttarakhand (Part-III). 2012. Accessed   25.06.2012. Available: http://agropedia.iitk.ac.in/?q=node/4550

2. Maheswari, R., Ashok, K.R. and Prahadeeswaran, M. 2011. Precision Farming Technology, Adoption Decisions and Productivity of Vegetables in Resource-Poor Environments. *Agricultural Economics Research Review* 21: 415-424.

3. Mondal, P. and Tewari, V.K. 2007. Present status of precision farming: a review. *Int J Agric Res*, 2(1):1–10.

4. Mondal, P., Tewari, V. K., Rao, P. N. 2004. Scope of precision agriculture in India. In: Proc of international conference on emerging technologies in agricultural and food engineering, Kharagpur, India. PMS 101/6; 2004. p. 103.

5. Pinaki, M., Basu, M. and Bhadoria, P.B.S. 2011. Review of Precision Agriculture Technologies and Its Scope of Adoption in India. *American J. Exp. Agric.* 1(3): 49-68.

6. Shibusawa, S. 2002. Precision farming approaches to small farm agriculture. Agro-Chemicals Report. 2002;2(4):13-20.

7. Srinivasan, A. 2006, Handbook of precision agriculture: principles and applications. Binghamton, NY: The Haworth Press; 2006.

Chapter-6

PROCESSING OF WATERMELON AND EXTRACTION OF BIOACTIVE COMPOUNDS

Hradesh Rajput, Pratistha Srivastav

Department of Food Technology, ITM, University, Gwalior, MP

and

Deepika Goswami

Central Institute of Post Harvest Engineering and Technology, Ludhiana, Punjab

ABSTRACT

Watermelon is a tropical fruit. In India watermelon is developed nearly consistently. Melons are gathered by natural product estimate, substance shading, and with or without seeds. The most commonly seen watermelons in the U.S. are seeded, seedless, mini, yellow, and orange melons. Dark red-fleshed, black seeded varieties are the most popular on the market place. "Seedless" melons, although more difficult to grow, have become popular in the market. Watermelon is found to contribute significantly to human health. It contains nutrients A, C, B6 and potassium. It is without fat, and high in sugar and water. Red fleshed watermelons are a great wellspring of lycopene. In India watermelon is used for making fresh juice, squash, flavor drinks, pickles and jelly etc. the extraction and filtration of lycopene is basic to utilize it in drugs, supplements, sustenance fixings and healthy skin creams and so forth.

Keywords: watermelon, lycopene, sugars, bioactive compounds and processing.

1. Introduction

Watermelon (Citrulluslanatus) is a tropical natural product, has a place with family Cucurbitaceae is a blossoming plant. It is a natural product, which is an exceptional kind alluded by botanists as a pepo, a berry that has a thick skin (exocarp) and tissue mesocarp and endocarp. Pepos are gotten from a mediocre ovary and are normal for the Cucurbitaceae. Watermelon begins from Africa, yet the precise topographical source and taming procedure of the harvest watermelon aren't clear. One likely quality focus is in the Kalahari Desert area where the species can even now be found in the wild in different structures. Presently, China is the world leader in watermelon production with 70.3% of total production in 2005. Other driving nations are Turkey (4.7%), Iran (2.3%), United States (2.2%) and Egypt (1.7%). India (290,485 mt) involves 26th position in watermelon generation. Watermelons were conveyed to China around the 10th century and afterward toward the Western Hemisphere not long after the disclosure of the New World. In Russia, where a significant part of the business supply of watermelons is developed, there is a well-known wine produced using this organic product.

Watermelon develops well in alluvial and sandy soils even in dry districts and seaside saline territories. In the Gangetic fields, early sowing is done in November and stretched out up to February; in South and Central, India watermelon is developed nearly consistently. The watermelon natural product, approximately thought about a sort of melon in spite of the fact that not in the family, Cucumis has a smooth outside skin (green, yellow and once in a while light green) and a delicious, sweet inside tissue (typically pink, yet now and then orange, yellow, red and here and there green if not ready). There are more than 1,200 assortments of watermelon worldwide accessible for planting. Watermelons are gathered by natural product estimate, substance shading, and with or without seeds. The most usually observed watermelons in the U.S. are seeded, seedless, and smaller than usual, yellow, and orange melons. Dark red-fleshed, dark seeded assortments are the most well known available spot. Yellow fleshed melons and small mini melons also find a ready market. "Seedless" melons, although more difficult to grow, have become popular in the market. Summer is the best time to eat watermelon because the harvest season in South Carolina is from May to August. Harvesting usually begins 3-4 months after planting. Maturity is sometimes difficult to determine. Watermelons do not store well as they are susceptible to chilling injury, and are subject to decay at higher temperatures. Watermelon should be cooled to between 12-15°C within 24 hours of harvesting if they are to be stored for long periods of time. They should be held at 10°C to 15°C and 90% relative humidity. Watermelon rinds are also edible and sometimes used as a fresh vegetable. In China, they are stir-fried, stewed, or more often pickled. Pickled watermelon rind is also commonly consumed in the Southern US, Russia, Ukraine, Romania, and Bulgaria. Fresh watermelon may be eaten in a variety of ways and is also often used to flavor drinks and smoothies (National watermelon Promotion Board Jul. 17, 2005). In India watermelon is used for making fresh juice, squash, flavor drinks, pickles, and jelly, etc. It is found to contribute significantly to human health. As with many other fruits, it is a source of vitamins A, C, B6, and potassium. It is fat-free, and high in energy. Watermelon contains about 6.2% sugar and 91.45% water by weight, red-fleshed watermelons are an excellent source of lycopene shown in Table 1.Red-fleshed melons contain 4,532 µg/100g lycopene. Lycopene is the compound that is responsible for the red color of watermelon.

Carotenoids are gainful in cardiovascular wellbeing, because of their extraordinary structure, secure tissues against oxidative and photooxidative harm by free radicals or receptive oxygen species created because of the metabolic and obsessive procedures. Carotenoids have cell reinforcement properties and potential medical advantages, choosing assortments with high centralization of carotenoids is significant for reproducing lines. Carotenoids might be accessible from the eating routine and assimilated, processed, or used by the human body. Watermelon is an esteemed wellspring of normal cancer prevention agents with extraordinary reference to the lycopene, ascorbic acid, and citrulline. These utilitarian fixings go about as security against perpetual medical issues like disease uprising and cardiovascular issue. Diets wealthy in carotenoids can avert cell harm, untimely skin maturing, and skin malignant growth.

Lycopene is a significant carotenoid color found in ready watermelon organic products. Lycopene may hinder the development of prostate tumors, give securing impacts to keep up prostate wellbeing and lower the danger of lung malignancy in humans. Lycopene is a bioactive red shading color normally happening in plants. Lycopene-rich nourishment is conversely related to illnesses, for example, malignant growths, cardiovascular ailments, diabetes and other maladies. Lycopene is fat-soluble and well-absorbed if applied externally (e.g. in a cream or lotion). In this manner, lycopene is a basic nutraceutical aggravate that gives critical wellbeing and health advantages.

Table 1. Nutritional composition per 100 g of fresh tomato

Parameters	Quantity
Water	91.45g
Carbohydrate	3.55g or 3%
Sugars	6.2g
Fat	0.15g
Protein	0.61g
Energy	127kg (30 cal)
Dietary fiber	0.4g or 2%
Ash content	2.85%
Lycopene	4532µg

The extraction and sanitization of lycopene is fundamental to utilize it in medications, supplements, nourishment fixings and healthy skin creams and so on. The neighborhood assortments of watermelon are effectively accessible in the market. Keeping in view the nutraceutical significance of lycopene the substance and nature of lycopene in watermelon to produce helpful data on subjective and quantitative parts of lycopene from this organic product.

1. Processing of watermelon

Different processed products are given below using watermelon

1.1 Watermelon Pulp-In-Juice Suspension

The way toward getting ready industrially sterile watermelon mash in-Juice suspension from the red mash of the watermelon, which contains expelling the red mash from the watermelon, smashing the equivalent to a fluid, having roughly 0.06% to 0.27% of fine red mash solids in suspension in the juice, including a frail natural corrosive in amount of about 0.2% to 0.4% to the mash in-juice suspension to bring the pH thereof in any event as low as generously pH 4.0 yet not as low as pH 3.0 and sanitizing the mash in juice suspension at temperature 1000C, whereby the last item is gotten, having the common red shading.

Fig. 1: Watermelon Pulp-In-Juice Suspension

1.2 Watermelon Juice (Ready To Serve)

Watermelon is washed and peeled by peeler. After peeling it is passed through the juice extractor to extract the juice. Strain the juice through the muslin cloth and analyzed for Brix^0, pH, and acidity (AOAC, 1984). 10% watermelon juice, 10% TSS and 0.3% acid are required in the final product. Prepared RTS is pasteurized at 80^{0}C for 5 min and hot fill in the glass bottles sealed it tightly. Bottles are sterilized at 100^{0}C for 20 min. The processed juice can be stored either at refrigerated conditions (4-5°C) or ambient conditions. The shelf life of beverage is 6 months at ambient condition and 12 months at refrigerated conditions.

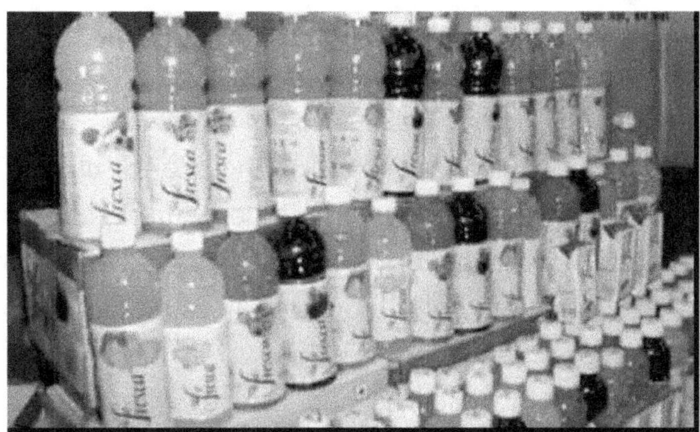

Fig. 2: Watermelon Juice (Ready To Serve)

1.3 Watermelon Squash

Watermelon is washed and peeled by peeler. After peeling it is passed through the juice extractor to extract the juice. The juice is strained through the muslin cloth and analyzed for Brix^0, pH, and acidity. Sugar, citric acid and water are mixed and heated. The syrup is cooled slightly and filtered through a cloth. Extracted juice and syrup are mixed properly. In the final product 25% watermelon juice, 45% TSS and 1.5% acid are required. Colour is added to the squash should be fairly resistant to the action of sulfur dioxide. After mixing all the ingredients, a calculated amount of a chemical preservative (potassium metabisulphite) is added to the squash. The amount of sulfur dioxide in the final product should not be more than 350 ppm. The sterile glass bottles (250 ml capacity) are rinsed with hot water before filling them with the squash, leaving about 1.2 to 2.5 cm of headspace. The bottles are then closed with crown corks, which have been dipped in potassium metabisulphite solution to sterilize them. The bottles are washed, dried and labeled. Bottles are Stored in a cool and dry place for 1-1.5 years.

Watermelon Rind Pickles

- 3 quarts (about 6 pounds) watermelon rind
- ¾ cup of salt
- 3 quarts water
- 2 quarts (2 trays) ice cubes
- 9 cups of sugar
- 3 cups 5% vinegar, white
- 3 cups of water
- 1 tablespoon (about 48) whole cloves
- 6 cinnamon sticks, 1-inch pieces
- 1 lemon, thinly sliced, with seeds removed

Procedure: Trim the pink fragile living creature and external green skin from thick watermelon skin. Cut into 1-inch squares or extravagant shapes as wanted. Spread with a saline solution made by blending the salt with 3 quarts virus water. Include ice cubes. Let stand 3 to 4 hours. Drain, rinse in cold water. Cover with cold water and cook until fork-tender, about 10 minutes. Drain. Add sugar, vinegar, water, and flavors (tied in a perfect, flimsy, white fabric). Bubble 5 minutes and pour over the watermelon; include lemon slices. Stand overnight in the refrigerator. Heat watermelon in syrup to boiling and cook gradually for 60 minutes. Pack hot pickles freely into spotless, hot pint containers. To each jar add 1 piece of stick cinnamon from spice bag; cover with boiling syrup, leaving ½ inch headspace. Remove air bubbles and adjust headspace if needed. Wipe edges of containers with a hosed clean paper towel; alter two-piece metal canning lids. Processing is done in the boiling water-bath for 5 minutes.

Fig. 3: Watermelon Rind Pickles

1.4 Watermelon Rind Jam

Jam produced using watermelon rind (WMR) waste is demonstrating that watermelon waste from restaurants, food, and beverages processing lines are inadequately being reused. WMR is one of the significant strong wastes created by several restaurants, cottage fruit juice makers. This waste rind is not presently being utilized for any esteem added forms because of constrained research exercises concentrating on the conceivable transformation of the loss to other important items subsequently making it accessible for dumping as strong waste. Chemically WMR contains a large amount of water with promising levels of solid matters but devoid of the high content of soluble sugar. These attributes made it a suitable contender for the generation of top-notch jam. This tale utilization of WMR will in addition to other things diminish the measure of the waste disposed of, make more salary for ranchers, nourishment processors and all the more significantly decrease natural effects of the waste.

Preparation of Jam: Already prepared watermelon rind is processed into jams according to the Food and Agriculture Organization's guidelines with slight modification. Take 250g of the rind and boiled it for some time. Boiled watermelon rinds are grind in the grinder and add 200g of sugar. The mixture is heated to boiling and 2g of citric acid is added to improve the taste. For sensory evaluation, flavors added. Five g pectin is added as the rind doesn't form good jell. The produced jams are hot filled into sterilized glass bottles, closed and stored at room temperature $(25-32^0C)$.

Fig. 4: Watermelon Rind Jam

1.5 Watermelon Yoghurt

At first, fresh and fully ripe fruit watermelon is washed properly. Peels are removed with the help of a sharp knife and seeds are removed from watermelon manually. Fruit pulp extract by a pulper separately. At that point, organic product mash is a channel with clean fabric and homogenized with a homogenizer. Homogenized natural product pulp is then whitened at $80\pm1°C$ for 5 minutes. In the wake of cooling, mash kept at refrigeration temperature (4°C) in clean PET bottles independently until the preparation of yogurt.

Yogurt Preparation: Fresh whole milk is filtered to remove dirt if any in it and then boiled to reduce 15% of its initial volume. Amid boiling of milk 10% sugar is included and blended persistently by a stirrer to counteract the development of cream layer. Boiled milk is permitted to cool and when milk temperature is 42-43°C. Five percent previously treated fruit pulp (watermelon) added to the cup. Starter culture (1.5%) is added at 41°C temperature in the cup and then incubated at 37°C for 8-12 hours until complete card formation. Finally, yogurt samples are cooled and stored at refrigerated condition.

Fig. 5: Watermelon yogurt

1.6 Watermelon Powder

Microencapsulation is a useful technique which has been widely used to protect the functionality of food ingredients against chemical reactions mainly caused by oxygen, water or light. Microcapsule are small particles that contain an active agent or core material surrounded by a coating or shell made up of some materials including many polymers, gum, carbohydrates, fat and waxes.The Microcapsules can be produced by a large number of different Microencapsulation process such as spray drying, extrusion, freeze-drying, coacervation, co-crystallization, molecular inclusion, etc. Spray drying has been successful used in the food industry due to its continuous production, low cost and available equipment. The food and food ingredient industry have increased commercial interest in exploring innovative strategies for encapsulating bioactive compound.

1.7 Microencapsulation process

To produce the watermelon, powder a buchi mini spray dryer model B-90 is used. The experimental parameters are 180 and 90^{0}C as inlet and outlet temperatures of the drying air, respectively; atomization pressure of 7 bar; airflow rate of 700 L/h and feed flow rate of 34 ml/min. Arabic gum and maltodextrin (DE=19-22), at 8% concentration each is used for encapsulating agents. The final total solid content of the feed mixture is 22%. The mixture is homogenized using a domestic blender. The obtained microcapsules are packed in aluminum bags and stored at room temperature. The Microencapsulation yield of the process (MY) is described as the ratio between the quality of dry powder (M) and the total solids (TS) of the feed solution according to the equation, these results are presented as percentage (%). The Microcapsules are stored for 15 days at room temperature in order to study the stability of lycopene and antioxidant capacity of the watermelon power.

$$MY\ (\%) = \frac{M}{TS} \times 100$$

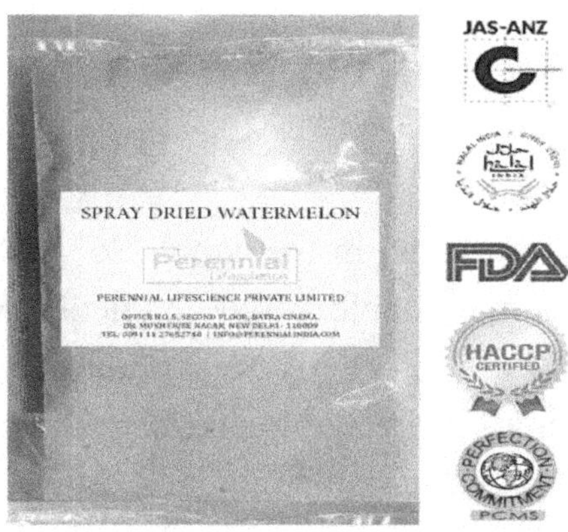

Fig. 6: Spray dried watermelon powder

1.8 Extraction of bioactive compounds

Watermelon is rich in lycopene, extraction and filtration of lycopene is fundamental to utilize it in meds, supplements, nourishment fixings and healthy skin creams etc. The local varieties of watermelon are effectively accessible in the market. Keeping in view the nutraceutical significance of lycopene, this investigation was embraced to assess the substance and nature of lycopene in watermelon to create helpful data on subjective and quantitative parts of lycopene from watermelon.

Methods of Lycopene Extraction

A process for isolating and purifying lycopene crystals from a biological lycopene source. A lycopene-containing oleoresin was saponified in a synthesis of propylene glycol and watery salt to form lycopene crystals. Crystallization was accomplished without using organic solvents. The crystals were detached and purified. The generously unadulterated pure lycopene crystals were reasonable for human utilization and could be utilized as a nourishing enhancement and as an added substance in different food product preparation. Used supercritical fluid extraction (SFE) of refrigerator dried watermelon tissue with CO_2 to extract lycopene. Preliminary studies have shown an ethanol modifier to be more effective in extracting lycopene. A unique procedure to extract lycopene from watermelon related to this research is described. Red watermelon flesh is ground and homogenized using a homogenizer. The ground flesh is then filtered through Mira cloth under vacuum. Filtrates from the filtration were subsequently passed through a centrifuge to precipitate lycopene. Samples for lycopene and sugar analysis were taken at appropriate steps during the process and then analyzed using a spectrophotometer and high-performance liquid chromatography (HPLC) respectively. The combined filtration processing and filtrate precipitation steps represent a means of concentrated watermelon lycopene into two fractions: a filter cake and filtrate pellet with a combined mass of less than 10% of the original melon weight. Lycopene recovery varied from 35-55% depending on maturity.

2. Quality Analysis Of Watermelon Using Different Methods

2.1 Antioxidant activity (DPPH assay)

The samples are more soluble in water and in methanol. So, these were utilized for DPPH test. The purple shaded DPPH is a stable free radical, which is decreased to 2, 2-diphenyl-1-picrylhydrazyl (yellow color) by responding with an antioxidant [30]. A concentration of 1mg/ml was setup by including 0.02 g sample in 20 ml distilled water or methanol. This spectrophotometer uses the stable radical 2, 2-Diphenyl-1-picrylhydrazyl (DPPH) as a reagent. Sample (100µl) was added to 3 ml of DPPH reagent. After 30 min incubation period at room temperature, the absorbance was showing against blank at 517 nm. The percentage inhibition of free radical (DPPH) was calculated as under:

Inhibition % (DPPH) = (Ablank -A sample/ Ablank) x 100 Where, A=Absorbance.

Fig. 6: Spectrophotometer

2.2 Acetone-petroleum ether extraction

Sample (1.0-1.5 g powder) is extracted with 10mL acetone petroleum ether (50% v/v). The upper lycopene-containing natural layer is evacuated by methods for a pipette and collected in a test tube. The same process is proceeding again. The concentrates are consolidated, washed with 15mL saturated aqueous sodium chloride (NaCl) and expelled the fluid wash with a micropipette. The concentrate is washed with 10mL of 10% aqueous potassium carbonate (K_2CO_3) and evacuated the fluid wash. The lycopene-containing natural layer is dried with a drying specialist (calcium chloride). The abundance of solvent is permitted to dissipate at room temperature for a couple of minutes in obscurity. The cylinders containing lycopene extricates are secured with aluminum foil and put in the freezer until further examination.

2.3 Hexane extraction

Sample (0.3 to 0.6 g powder) is weighed in a beaker, 5 ml BHT acetone solution (0.05%, w/v), 5 ml ethanol and 10 ml hexane is added. The beaker is placed in a bowl of ice on a magnetic stirring plate, stirred for 15 min and added 3 ml distilled water. It is shaken for 5 min on ice and incubated at room temperature for 5 min to allow the separation of both layers. The upper layer containing lycopene is confined by methods for a pipette and put in a test tube. The cylinders containing lycopene separates are secured with aluminum foil and put away in the refrigerator until further analysis.

2.4 UV-VIS Spectrophotometer

The absorbance value at 503nm is used for the determination of lycopene content in tomato, cherry tomatoes, and watermelon. In one quartz cuvette (1 cm optical path), hexane is used as blank. Three absorbance values are obtained. The results are determined by the equation (Beer-Lambert law). Absorbance values of four fractions obtained by column chromatography are noted at 360, 443, 471 and 503nm.

$$\textit{Lycopene content (mg/kg)} = \textit{Absorbance} \times 31.2$$

Column chromatography Lycopene obtained by acetone-petroleum ether extraction from tomato, cherry tomato and watermelon is purified by column chromatography using Plastic column (20ml). Alumina (Grade II) is used as adsorbent. Lycopene sample is added to the prepared column. The column is filled with the solvent and the sample is eluted from the column. Firstly, the yellow carotene band is eluted by hexane. The eluting solvent is switched to 10% acetone-hexane to elute the lycopene from the column.

2.5 Thin Layer Chromatography (TLC)

TLC is performed on unrefined lycopene (obtained by extraction) and pure lycopene (obtained by column chromatography). Silica plates (MERCK) are set up by illustration a pencil line 1 cm from the base of the TLC plate. Samples are spotted using glass spotters. The organic solvent (9:1 petroleum ether and dichloromethane) is used. TLC plate is set in the tank for 5-10 min. The edge of the plate is set apart to demonstrate how far the dissolvable went up the plate. TLC plate is dried in the hood, the colors are set apart with a pencil and the plate is examined under UV light.

Rf value = distance from origin to component spot (cm)/ distance from origin to solvent front (cm)

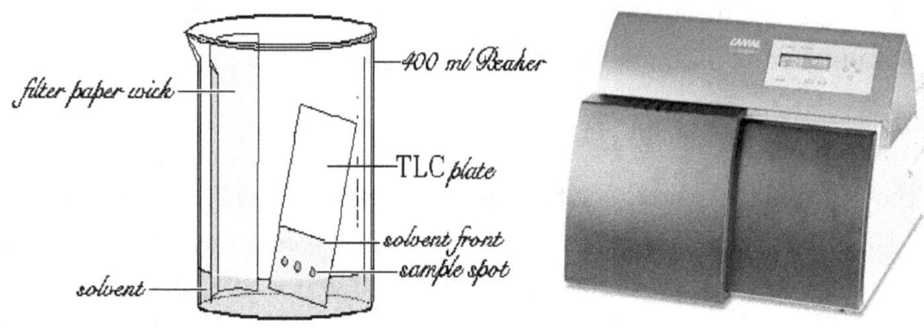

Fig. 7: Thin Layer Chromatography (TLC)

2.6 Fourier Transform Infrared (FTIR) Spectroscopy

Fourier Transform Infrared (FTIR) Spectroscopy is performed on purified lycopene samples. FTIR Spectrometer (BRUKER, Germany) is used. The liquid samples are sandwiched between two plates. The plates are transparent to the infrared light and do not introduce any lines onto the spectra. Standard spectra of the samples are collected individually.

Conclusion

The antioxidant activity of watermelon is measured in water and methanol extracts. These fruits vary in antioxidant activity; however, high activity is recorded in watermelon. The aqueous solution is found to be better solvent than methanol for antioxidant activity of these fruits. Acetone-petroleum ether extraction is found better for high lycopene yield than hexane extraction. Purified lycopene can be easily obtained through single column purification. Watermelon exhibited high lycopene contents indicating that lycopene is major contributor of antioxidant capacities of these fruits. The results of the present study suggests that these fruits contained potential antioxidant bioactive compounds particularly lycopene, which if properly utilized could provide a source of biologically active nutraceutical ingredient/ medicine application. It also shows its titanic importance as a therapeutic agent in preventing or curing the diseases caused due to oxidative stress.

References

1. Van der Vossen HAM, Denton OA, El Tahir, IM (2004). Citrulluslanatus (Thunb.) Matsum. And Nakai. In Grubben GJH, Denton OA (eds) Plant Resources of Tropical Africa, Vegetables. PROTA Foundation, Wageningen, Netherlands/Backhuiser Publishers, Leiden /CTA, Wageningen, Netherlands, pp. 185-191.

2. Zohary, D, Hopf M, Weiss E. Domestication of plants in the old world: The origin and spread of domesticated plants in Southwest Asia, Europe, and the Mediterranean Basin. 4th ed. Oxford: Oxford Univ. Press, 2012.

3. Lucier G, Lin B-H. Factors affecting watermelon consumption in the United States. In: USDA, United States Department of Agriculture (Ed.): Vegetables and specialties: situation and outlook report, VGS287;2001:23-9.

4. Naz A, Butt MS, Pasha I, Nawaz H. (2013). Antioxidant indices of watermelon juice and lycopene extract. Pak J Nutr. 12:255-60.

5. Davis AR, Collins JK, Fish WW, Webber III CL, Perkins-Veazie P, Tadmor YK. A rapid hexane-free method for analyzing total carotenoid content in canary yellow-fleshed watermelon. In: Cucurbitaceae: Proceedings, Asheville, North Carolina. September 17-21, 2006; p. 545-552.

6. Kraemer K, Packer L, Sies H, and Ute O-J. Carotenoids and Retinoids: Molecular Aspects and Health Issues. Illinois, USA: AOCS Publishing. AOCS Press Champaign; 2005.

7. Dembinska-Kiec A. Carotenoids: risk or benefit for health. Biochimicaet Biophysica Acta 2005; 1740: 93-94.

8. Davis AR, Fish WW, Perkins-Veazie P.A rapid Hexane-free method for analyzing lycopene content in watermelon. Journal of Food science 2003; 68 (1): 328-332.

9. Khachik F. 2004. Chemical and Metabolic Oxidation of Carotenoids. Oxidants and antioxidants in biology: A conference organized by the Oxygen Club of California (OCC) and co-sponsored by the Linus Pauling Institute. Fess Parker's Double Tree Resort Santa Barbara, California. 10-13 March, 2004.

10. Zhang D, Hamauzu Y. Phenolic compounds and their antioxidant properties in different tissues of carrots (Daucuscarota L.). J Food Agric Environ 2004; 2:95100.

11. Omoni AO, Aluko RE. The anti-carcinogenic and anti-atherogenic effects of lycopene: a review. Trends Food Sci. Technol. 2005; 16:344-50.

12. Fenko A, Schifferstein HN, Huang TC, Hekkert P. What makes products fresh: The smell or the colour? Food Qual Prefer 2009; 20:372-9.

13. Shi J, Le Maguer M, Bryan M. Lycopene from Tomatoes in Functional Foods: Biochemical and Processing Aspects. CRC Press, Boca Raton. 2002.

14. Obermuller-Jevic U, Olano-Martin E, Weerden WV, Kramer K, Cross CE, Schroder FH, Packer L. Lycopene and Prostate Health. Oxidants and antioxidants in biology: A conference organized by the Oxygen Club of California (OCC) and co-sponsored by the Linus Pauling Institute. Fess Parker's Double Tree Resort Santa Barbara, California. March 10-13, 2004.

15. Stacewicz-Sapuntzakis M, Bowen PE. Role of lycopene and tomato products in prostate health. Biochimicaet Bio-physica Acta 2005; 1740: 202-205.

16. Wang X-D. Biological activity of lycopene against smoke-induced lung lesions. Oxidants and antioxidants in biology: A conference organized by the Oxygen Club of California (OCC) and co-sponsored by the Linus Pauling Institute. Fess Parker's Double Tree Resort Santa Barbara, California. March 10-13, 2004.

17. Kong KW, Khoo HE, Prasad KN, Ismail A, Tan CP, Rajab NF. Revealing the power of the natural red pigment lycopene. Molecules 2010: 15 (2): 959-987.

18. Chauhan K, Sharma S, Agarwal N, Chauhan B. Lycopene of tomato fame: its role in health and disease. International Journal of Pharmaceutical Sciences Review and Research 2011; 10 (1): 99-115.

19. AOAC, 1984.Official Methods of Analysis of the Association of Official Analytical Chemists.14th edition Arlington, Virginia, USA.

20. Souad, A.M., Jamal, P. and Olorunnisola, K. S. 2012. Effective jam preparations from watermelon waste. International Food Research Journal 19(4): 1545-1549.

21. FAO STAT (2008). Crops. FAOSTAT. Food and agriculture organization of the united nations. (Database).

22. Debashis Kumar Dutta Roy, Tanny Saha1, Moriom Akter, Mojaffor Hosain, Habiba Khatun and Manik Chandra Roy 2015. Quality Evaluation of Yogurt Supplemented with Fruit Pulp (Banana, Papaya, and Water Melon). International Journal of Nutrition and Food Sciences 2015; 4(6): 695-699.

23. Jimenez, M., Garcia, H.S. and beristain, C.I. 2004. Spray drying Microencapsulation and oxidative stability of conjugative lenolaic acid. Europ. Food Res. Technol. 219:588-592.

24. Re, R., Pellegrini, N., Proteggnte, A., Pannala, A., Yang, M. and Rice evans, C. 1999. Antioxidant activity applying an improved abts radical cationdecolorization assay. Free radical Biology & Medicine 26(9/10):1231-1237.

25. Gouin, S. 2004. Micro-encapsulation: Industrial appraisal of existing technologies and trends. Trends of food Sci. Techno. 15: 330-347.

26. Rodriguez-Amaya, D.B. 2002. Brazil: a boundy of carotenoid source. Campinas: Newsletter/Sight and life 4:3-9.

27. Ausich, R. L. and S. J. David. 1999. Process for the isolation and purification of lycopene crystals. U.S. Patent No. 5858700

28. Vaughn, K. L. S., D. J. Carrier, L. R. Loward and E. C. Clausen. 2003. Extraction of lycopene from watermelon. In Proc. IFT annual meeting, 76B-16. Chicago, IL.

29. Maness, N. O., I. P. Oikonomakos, D. Chrz, P. Perkins-Veazie. 2002. A novel procedure for lycopene recovery from red-fleshed watermelons. In Proc. FAPC research symposium.

30. Ivanišová E, Tokár M, Mocko K, Bojňanská T, Mareček J, Mendelová A. Antioxidant activity of selected plant products. Journal of Microbiology, Biotechnology and Food Sciences 2013; 2: 692-1703.

31. Brand-Williams W, Cuvelier ME, Berset C. Use of free radical method to evaluate antioxidant activity. LWT Food Science and Technology 1995; 28 (1): 25-30.

32. Lehman JW. Operational organic chemistry. A problem-solving approach to the laboratory course.4th ed. Prentice Hall. 2009.

33. Ravelo-pérez LM, Hernández-borges J, Rodríguez-delgado MA, Borges-miquel T. Spectrophotometric analysis of lycopene in tomatoes and watermelons: A Practical Class. The Chemical Educator 2008; 13(1).

34. Souza MCD, Singha S, Ingle M. Lycopene Concentration of Tomato Fruit can be estimated from Chromaticity Values. Plant and Soil 1992; 27 (5): 465-466.

35. Naviglio D, Pizzolongo F, Ferrara L, Arag A, Santini A. Extraction of pure lycopene from industrial tomato by-products in water using a new high-pressure process. Journal of the Science of Food and Agriculture 2008; 88 (14): 2414-2420.

36. Vasta JD, Sherma J. Analysis of lycopene in nutritional supplements by silica gel high-performance thin-layer chromatography with visible-mode densitometry. Acta Chromatographica 2008; 20 (4): 673-683.

37. Bunghez IR, Raduly M, Doncea S, Aksahin I, Ion RM. Lycopene determination in tomatoes by different spectral techniques (UV-VIS, FTIR and HPLC). Journal of Nanomaterials 2011; 6 (3): 1349-1356.

Chapter -7

MOLECULAR AND PHYSIOLOGICAL CHARACTERIZATION OF PLANT GROWTH PROMOTING RHIZOBACTERIA: METHODS AND PROTOCOLS

Abhijeet Shankar Kashyap[1], Meenakshi Tetorya[2,] Amit Kumar Kesharwani[3], NaziaManzar[5], Ravinder Pal Singh[1], Thungri ghoshal[1], Chander Mani[1], and Dinesh Singh[6]*

[1,3,6]*IndianAgricultural Research Institute,New Delhi, India*
[1,5]*National Bureau of Agriculturally important microorganisms Mau, Uttar Pradesh, India*
[2]*University of Delhi, South Campus, New Delhi, India*

ABSTRACT

Fifty years ago, the green revolution increased agricultural production worldwide, saving millions of people from starvation and undernourishment. To enhance plant growth and nutrition, plant growth-promoting rhizobacteria (PGPR) plays a significant role in the intensively managed agricultural systems. The rising demand for crop production with a significant reduction in synthetic chemical fertilizers and pesticide use is a challenge. Plant growth-promoting rhizobacteria (PGPR) are those microorganisms that live within a rhizospheric zone of plant host in a symbiosis relationship. PGPRis beneficial microorganism to plant that can protect it from deleterious effects of environmental stresses such as drought, salinity, flooding, and phytopathogens. The mechanisms of PGPR include curbing hormonal and nutritional harmony, inducing systemic resistance against phytopathogens, and solubilizing nutrients for easy uptake by crops. Molecular tools showed great potential in the identification and tracking of the phylogeny of soil microbes. Today is the era of omics which including genomics, transcriptomics, proteomics and metabolomics, these omics helps us to the better understanding of the PGPRs function and their interaction with the host. Proteomics enhances the knowledge of the gene(s) and pathways induced during the host-PGPR interaction. The 2D-PAGE strategy has been widely used in understanding stress responses as well as in understanding constitutive differences between developmental stages or genotypes. First, it provides a broad overview of proteins produced by both the partners. Second, it allows the detection of signal transduction pathways and post-translational modifications of proteins, which decides the function of the protein. Bioinformatics tool helps in silico gene prediction that can be used for disease management, of their diverse uses in agriculture and environmental sustainability, the Knowledge of PGPRs, their characterization and identification is crucial to understand the distribution and diversity of indigenous bacteria in the rhizosphere. The isolated PGPR strains were characterized by their morphological, cultural and biochemical properties. Morphological characters include the colour and shape of the colony and the presence or absence of the capsule. The Gram staining of each isolate was initially determined followed by the biochemical characterization (catalase, oxidase, citrate utilization, H_2S production, KOH test). These efficient PGPR strains directly involved in the enhancement of plant growth by utilizing various kinds of mechanisms such as Biological nitrogen fixation (BNF), siderophores production, solubilization of minerals including phosphorus, increased absorption of nitrogen, phosphorus, potassium and induces the hyper synthesis of phytohormones such as indole acetic acid (IAA), gibberellic acid (GA3) and antifungal activity. The number of molecular approaches has also been used for the identification of PGPRs, including Random Amplification of Polymorphic DNA, 16S rDNA, and nif H gene amplification. The *in-silico* approaches have also been proven the great applicability in the identification of novel genes from unidentified isolates of PGPRs.

Keywords: PGPRs, Omics, Rhizosphere, rhizobacteria, nitrogen fixation

1. Introduction

Rhizosphere, the upper thin layer of soil provides habitat to diverse kinds of microorganisms including bacteria, fungi, protozoa, algae that exert positive as well as negative impacts on plants. This layer of soil is the narrow zone and is rich in nutrients for microbes compared to the bulk of soil, as it is a chemically complex environment where rhizobacteria contribute to maximum part to soil microflora. Aclass of bacteria play an influential role in maintaining soil fertility, plant growth and development are called rhizobacteriaThese rhizobacteria are called as plant growth-promoting rhizobacteria (PGPR), coined by Kloepper and Schroth in 1978. The PGPRs interact with the plants either by symbiosis or as free-living bacteria. They are capable to colonize in a rhizospheric zone of plants and help to stimulate the key compounds which help to the development of plant along with an increase in the crop productivity.

These efficient PGPR strains directly involved in the enhancement of plant growth by utilizing various kinds of mechanisms such as Biological nitrogen fixation (BNF),siderophores production for better plant health, solubilization of minerals including phosphorus, increased absorption of nutrients like nitrogen, phosphorus, potassium, and induces hyper synthesis of phytohormones such as indole acetic acid (IAA), and gibberellin (GA_3) acid and antifungal activity. Being a group of free-living significant soil bacteria with diverse functions PGPRs make crucial part of the biosphere and an absolute requirement for sustainable agriculture and environment. Previous studies have demonstrated their role in suppression of root pathogenicity and enhancement of plant growth by direct inoculation of some = PGPRs strain in the soil. Many PGPR strains *i.e.Azoarcus, Pseudomonas, Azospirillum, Azotobacter, Arthrobacter, Bacillus, Clostridium, Burkholdaria, Enterobacter, Gluconacetobacter, Rhizobium, Erwinia, Mycobacterium, Mesorhizobium, Flavobacterium,* etc. have already been reported to have a direct role in plant growth promotion (PGP) for sustainable development of crops. The direct inoculation of PGPR strains such as *Pseudomonas flseudomona* and *Azotobacter* has shown much improvement in overall plant growth and crop yield. Recently, Kumar et al. have demonstrated the effect of PGPRs on the growth and yield of wheat. Similarly, fungus-like *Trichoderma* spp. has been considered as one of the efficient bio-control agents against several plants and soil pathogenic fungi, used for plant disease control. Because, of their diverse uses in agriculture and environmental sustainability, the knowledge of PGPRs, their characterization, and identification is crucial to understand the distribution and diversity of indigenous bacteria in the rhizosphere. A combination of both physiological and molecular approaches can prove to be useful for studying microbial diversity within different genera. Physiological characterization of PGPRs is based on their use as biostimulant, biofertilizer and bioprotectant for the growth of plants and their protection against soil-borne pathogens. A number of molecular approaches have also been used for the identification of PGPRs, including Random Amplification of Polymorphic DNA, 16S rDNA and nif H gene amplification. The in-silico approaches have also been proven the great applicability in the identification of novel genes from unidentified isolates.

1.1 Molecular characterization of PGPRs

Molecular tools showed great potential in the identification and tracking of the phylogeny of soil microbes. Considerable reports are available on molecular-based approaches that can be used for detailed insight for PGPRs and other microorganisms.

1.2 Genomics

Genomics deals with the full genome of an organism that constitutes the application of recombinant DNA technologies, gene sequencing methods and bioinformatics for sequencing, assembling and analyses of the functions and structures of genomes.

1.2.1. Random Amplification of polymorphic DNA (RAPD)

Random amplification of polymorphic DNA has been known as a very promising tool for the identification of the PGPR strains as there is no requirement of prior sequence information. RAPD has been described by Williams et al. 1990. It is a kind of PCR amplification reaction but the amplicons obtained by this method are usually random. Previous reports have been described the importance of RAPD analysis in the evaluation of genetic diversity in soil microflora

(Saharan and Nehra, 2011).The utility of RAPD for the estimation of genetic diversity of PGPRs have been shown by Shaheen et al. 2015.

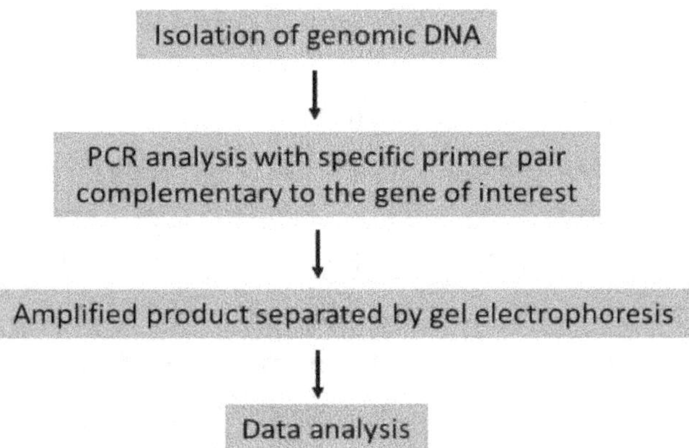

Fig. 1: Schematic representation of steps involved in RAPD technique.

This approach has been inutile for the genetic analysis of *Bacillus* isolates, identification of an Italian *Rhizobium meliloto* isolates and characterization of *Burkholderiacepacia* population by voluminous researchers.This tool has been extensively used as a molecular marker for deducing the genetic diversity of the number of PGPRs. The utmost attraction of this technique is the use of a small amount of DNA without the requirement of cloning and sequencing burden on the researcher. There are important steps involved in the whole procedure can be described in fig.1.

1.2.1.1 Data interpretation for RAPD analysis: Data analysis of RAPD involves the scoring of presence (1) or absence (0) of polymorphic bands in individual lanes on an agarose gel. Scoring on the banding profiles can be clear and transparent but in some cases, scoring can be difficult if the gel is blurred.

1.2.1.2. DNA polymorphisms among individuals: DNA polymorphisms among different individuals can be accounted due to the mismatches at the primer sites, the appearance of new primer sites and length of amplified fragments between primer sites.

1.3.2. 16S Ribosomal RNA (rRNA) sequencing
The 16S rRNA sequencing approach is generally used for further authentication of results obtained by RAPD profiling. Majority of reports has documented the PCR screening of 16S rRNA gene from bacterial isolates. 16S rRNA genes were found to be highly conserved among all organisms and can be used as biological markers for identification of living organisms at the different levels of their organization i.e., species, genus and family level. Molecular

identification by 16S rRNA has been reported for Azotobacter, Trichoderma and many other crop-specific PGPRs. It is an amplicon sequencing tool generally used for the identification and comparison of different bacterial isolates including PGPRs present within the given sample. It is a well-established method for studying evolutionary origin and taxonomy of targeted samples from complex microbiome or environments that are difficult to study.

1.3.2.1. Homology search and phylogenetic analysis

Homology based studies involve data interpretation and analysis of sequencing obtained as a result of the sequencing of library clones. Gene sequences of library clones are compared with other available sequences in the GenBank databases using the NCBI. Gene sequences that show very high alignment scores are retrieved and aligned using Clustalx2 software. Phylogenetic trees are also constructed using neighbour-joining method with Clustalx2 software with bootstrap support. Basic workflow for 16S rRNA sequencing is given in Fig.2.

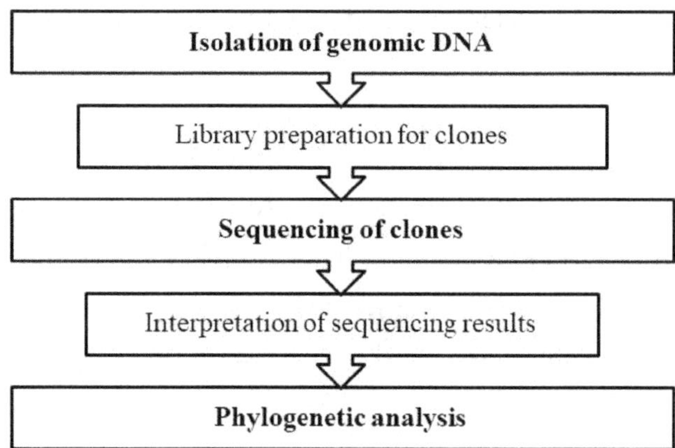

Fig. 2: Schematic representation of steps involved in 16S rRNA sequencing method

1.3.3 PCR amplification and molecular cloning of nif H gene

Identification of different classes of PGPRs was also performed by PCR screening of isolated bacterial DNA, amplification of nif H gene by using gene-specific forward and reverse primers and comparison of amplification products with expected sizes of nif H gene. The molecular characterization of nif H gene of diazotrophic growth-promoting bacteria from wheat rhizospheric soil performed by Gosal et al. 2011. The amplified PCR product of genes obtained in such experiments are confirmed on 1% agarose gel followed by the purification of PCR products through PCR purification kit and cloned into suitable TA cloning vector. Moreover, DNA from all plasmids is isolated and restriction digestions are performed with the desired restriction enzymes for the confirmation of putative transformed clones. Further, The DNA sequencing is used to confirm the transformed clones and their analyses as described earlier.

1.3.4. GFP (Green fluorescent protein) tagging

Many research findings are available which suggest the use of GFP gene to construct bacterial metal-biosensors and used for bio-augmentation of a metal-contaminated soil. The survival of PGPRs can be determined by analysis of plant inoculants which is tagged with a fluorescent marker for the better identification and monitoring (Fig.3). Additionally, The GFP tagging has been excessively suitable for the monitoring of rhizobacteria in soil and avoiding major disturbances to natural pattern of microflora colonization.

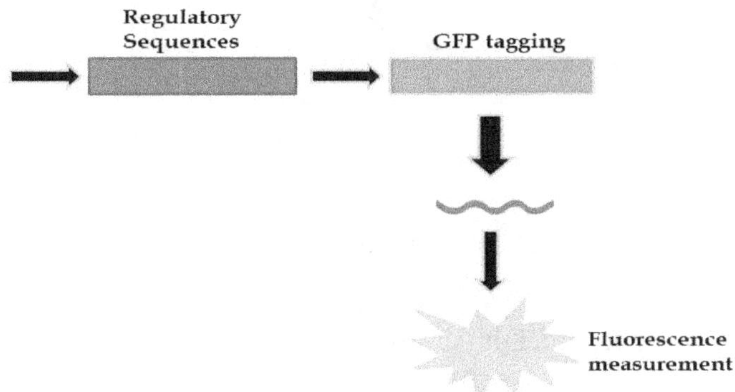

Fig. 3: The tagging of Green Fluorescence Protein for the identification of PGPRs

1.3.5. Next-generation sequencing technique (NGS)

Next-generation sequencing technology has revolutionized the molecular world by providing a potential tool for whole-genome sequencing of all organisms including microbiome. NGS has been employed to characterize and study genomes of several PGPRs. In addition to that PGPRs from soil have also been sequenced directly. Gupta et al. (2014) have reported whole-genome sequencing for the first time for the PGPRs isolated from coconut, cocoa and areca nut respectively. Sequencing of genomes was followed by the genome assembly and then the genome sizes are estimated and compared. Gupta and co-workers observed a good correlation between the genome sizes and genome numbers of the three PGPRs as shown in earlier reports.

1.3.5.1. Next-generation sequencing technique (NGS)

The essential steps of NGS can be divided into three broad categories:

1) **Library Preparation**: Libraries are created by random fragmentation of genomic DNA followed by ligation with custom linkers (Fig.4.).

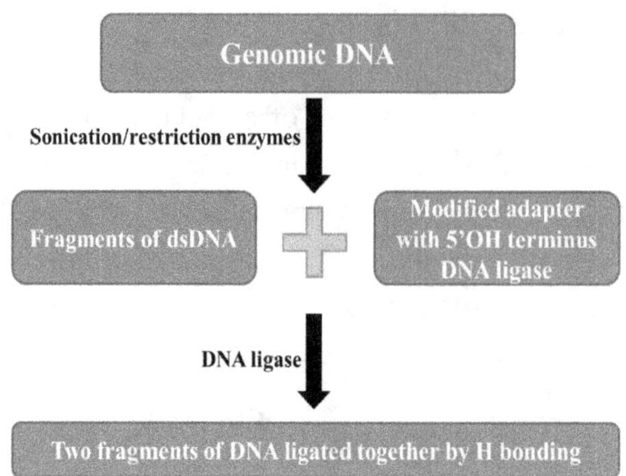

Fig. 4: Representation of library preparation for NGS data analyses

2) Amplification: Amplification of libraries accompanied by PCR reactions.

3) Sequencing: Amplified genomic DNAs are sequenced by using one of the several methods available and given below:

(i) Pyrosequencing

(ii) Reverse terminator sequencing (Illumina)

(iii) Ion-torrent semiconductor sequencing

(iv) Sequencing by ligation (SoLiD)

Despite the many applications of NGS there are certain limitations of these techniques as it results in generation of a huge amount of data which is associated with computational challenges.

1.3.5.2. Data interpretation and analysis of NGS

Data interpretation for NGS can be performed in following steps:

i. **Gene prediction:** Various bioinformatics programs are available for gene prediction analysis and can be used for the prediction of protein-coding genes.

ii. **Gene annotation:** To annotate the gene, the comparison of predicted protein-coding genes against non-redundant (nr) NCBI protein database using BLASTX. Moreover, Top hit database accession numbers are extracted from BLASTX results and these accession numbers then compared with Uniprot knowledgebase for annotating genes (Magrane and Consortium 2011). These annotating genes can be inspected for their involvement in various functions i.e., PGP functions, pathogen suppression, abiotic stress tolerance, rhizosphere competence, carbohydrate metabolism and other important relevant functions.

iii. **Phylogenetic analysis:** Phylogenetic studies are performed to identify evolutionary origin and relationship of relatively new identified strains with already existing strains of PGPRs and other bacterial isolates. There are various tools, software and online databases are available for the phylogenetic analysis and ClustalW2 is one of them and very imperative to the analysis of the phylogeny of relative strains.

iv. **Genome comparison:** The last step in NGS data analyses is the comparison of the whole assembled genome with the available complete genomes with the help of genome alignment tools.

Additionally, all the information obtained through whole-genome data analysis can be utilized to support the observed traits and making them ideal candidates for further development as bio-fertilizers as well as identified genes can be further studied for specific functions using knockout strategies.These molecular approaches thus can be used to further augment the plant growth-promoting properties of soil bacteria. The results obtained through molecular analysis can be used to design comprehensive strategies for development and utilization of PGPRs to support sustainable plantation and crop production.

1.4 Transcriptomics

The transcriptome is composed of messenger or coding RNAs and a variety of non-coding RNAs (ncRNAs) and it is dynamic and a good representative of the cellular state often uses high-throughput techniques based on DNA microarray technology. Expression analyses also involve the use of next-generation sequencing technology (already explained) to study the mRNA is known as RNA sequencing (RNA-Seq).

1.4.1 DNA Microarray

DNA Microarray technology is constantly evolving the method and used as an experimental tool for the identification of emerging PGPRs. DNA microarray can be classified into two basic types: cDNA microarray and oligonucleotide-based array. The DNA microarray technology is particularly suitable for profiling of gene expression of plant colonizing PGPRs due to relative simplicity, comprehensive sampling and high throughput (Schenk et al. 2000). Expression of thousands of genes can be examined simultaneously in a single experiment. Differential gene expression can be determined for different PGPRs during their colonization to plant roots.

1.4.1.2. cDNA Microarray

cDNA Microarray has basically involved the hybridization of thousands of genes from cDNA to their corresponding targets on a chip or filter. cDNA was prepared by reverse transcription of mRNA isolated from targeted bacterial strain via appropriate reverse transcriptase enzyme. Moreover, the current challenge for this technique is to analyze the huge amount of raw numerical data obtained in the form of hybridization signals. Thus, computational and bio-statistical analyses are required for acquiring significant information regarding differential gene expression of target genes under investigation.

1.4.1.3. Oligonucleotide array

Oligonucleotide based array technique is similar to cDNA microarray accept the use of oligo instead of cDNA on chips. The length of oligos usually depends on the application but they are no larger than 25 base pairs (bp). cDNA microarrays are often used for RNA expression analyses while oligonucleotide arrays can be additionally used for sequence analysis.

1.5. Proteomics

The term proteomics stands for large-scale analysis of proteins including their structure and functions. Knowledge-based on genomics and transcriptomics can only provide a list of genes without providing detailed insights into their functional significance but proteomics is able to give a full insight of genes and their pathways induced during host-PGPR interactions.

1.5.1. 2D-PAGE

The 2D gel electrophoresis deals with the separation of proteins and subsequent staining by Coomassie brilliant blue, and spots so obtained after electrophoresis are excised and identified using mass spectrometry. Molecules get separate in both the dimensions (1D and 2D) on the basis of their biochemical properties. The first-dimensional electrophoresis begins with the separation of molecules linearly according to their isoelectric point. In the second dimension, the molecules are then separated perpendicular to the first electropherogram according to their molecular mass. This approach has been exploited for understanding stress responses during plant-pathogen interactions and to study the differences between different genotypes. Gel-free proteomic systems are also under development that could be able to minimize the limitations associated with this technique. Proteomics-based tools have been used to identify proteins expressed in plant-bacterial interactions. This approach has been successfully employed by previous workers to identify proteins that are involved in the early stages of nodulation between the subterranean clover cultivar and Rhizobium. The 2D- gel electrophoresis has also been used in the model plant *Medicago truncatula*, inoculated either with the arbuscular mycorrhizal fungus *Glomus mosseae* or with the nitrogen fixing bacteria *Sinorhizobiummeliloti* for deducing root protein profiles in them. Peck et al. (2001) were able to identify proteins that are rapidly phosphorylated in the response of Arabidopsis cells to microbial elicitors and similarly a number of new pathogens and elicitor proteins have been identified with the help of proteomics-directed approach. Data generated through genomics and transcriptome analysis cannot be used to prove mechanisms concerned with gene regulation nor can they easily be distinguished between direct and indirect regulatory effects. These data can be complemented by proteomics. But there are also some voids with using proteomics as a solitary tool because of its association with major limitations such as 2D gel electrophoresis is unable to detect protein which is present in a cell in low abundance and can be important for cell-cycle regulation, signal transduction and functions as receptors. Thus, the combination of all "omics" is required to have proper insight into plant-microbe interactions and identification of novel PGPRs.

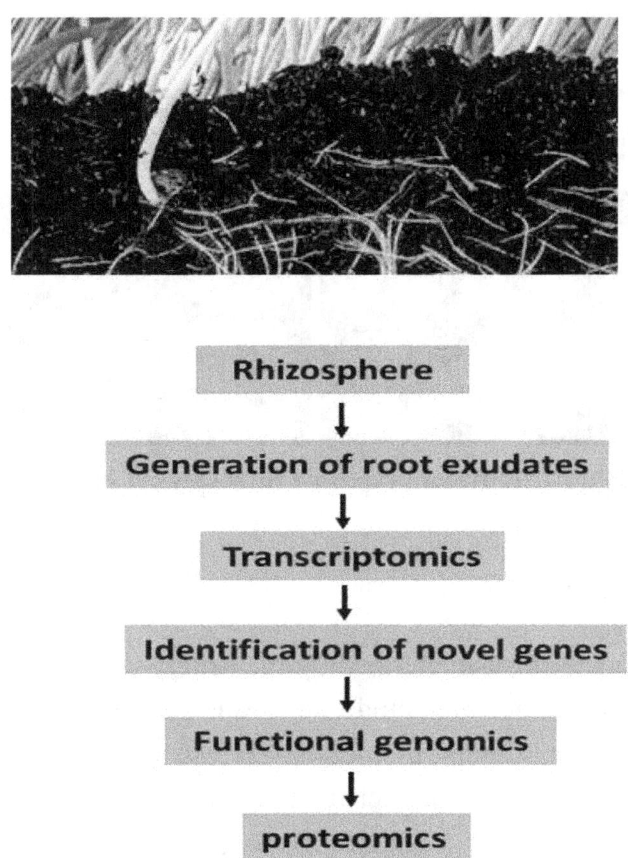

Fig. 6: A schematic diagram of different molecular techniques for identification of PGPRs

2. Physiological characterization of PGPRs

2.1 Collection and isolation of PGPR from soil sample

The soil from the plant root zone was taken as a sample ~ 10 g, was mixed with 100 mL of distilled water in a 500mL flask. The soil was mixed and heated at 80C for 15 min. 10 mL of suspension was taken and poured into 90mL of sterilized water and diluted up to 10-7 for all samples. Then 100 µL of diluted suspensions were taken at different concentration (10-3, 10-5, 10-7) and spread by using L- shaped glass rod on to different solid media plates (like King's media, TSA media, nutrient agar media and LA media). Incubate the plates for 36 hours at 28 ±1°C in BOD incubator.

2.2 Purification of the observed colony

After selecting the true colonies, transferred them on to the yeast glucose chalk agar media (YGCA) slants. Use a loop of the inoculation needle on a single colony and streaked it on agar slant in a tube, the cultures result from single colony isolation was need to undergo purity check. Makes a dilute suspension of the culture in water and streaked on nutrient agar plates.

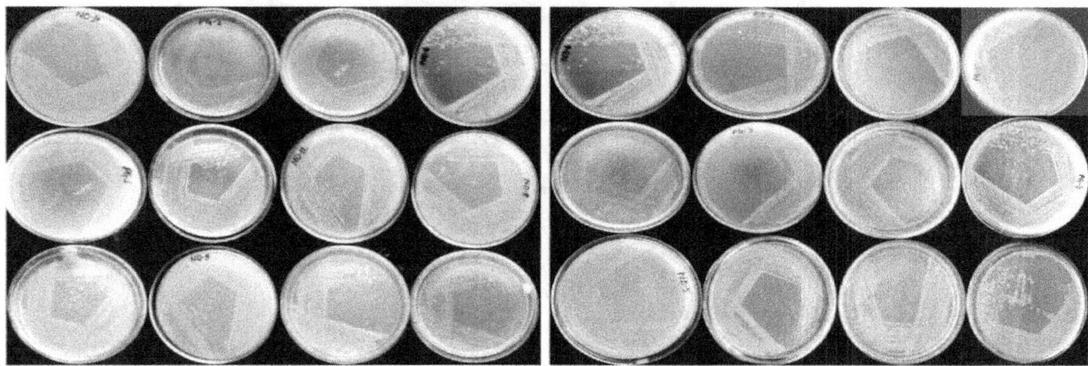

Fig. 7: Different types of rhizospheric bacteria

2.3 Characterization of PGPR

The isolated PGPR strains were characterized by their morphological, cultural and biochemical properties. Morphological characters include color and shape of the colony and presence or absence of capsule. The gram staining of each isolate was initially determined by using crystal violet and safranin stain. The biochemical characterization (catalase, oxidase, citrate utilization, H2S production, KOH test) of the isolates were performed by standard microbiological techniques.

2.3.1 Morphology test

2.3.1.1 KOH Test
Requirements: 24 hrs old culture of PGPR, Potassium hydroxide (KOH) (3% aq. w/v), inoculation loop and microscopic glass slide.

Procedure: 1-2 drop of 3% KOH was put onto a clean microscopic glass slide with a pipette. A 24 hrs old single colony of Rhizobacteria from slant was taken with the help of a sterile loop and mix loopful bacteria with KOH until an even suspension was obtained. The loop from the slide was lifted.

Observation: Gram-negative bacteria will become gummy upon mixing with a loop and a string of slime is lifted while gram-positive bacteria will not, and produce a watery suspension. If questionable results are obtained the gram stain should be used.

2.3.1.2. Gram staining

Requirements: 24 hrs old culture of *Rhizobacteria*, clean microscopic glass slide, glass rods, cotton, tape water, cleaning agent, microscopes, blotting sheets, Hucker's crystal violet, safranin, 95% ethyl alcohol, Gram's modification of Lugol solution.

Preparation of solution with chemical composition:

1. Hucker's ammonium oxalate crystal violet (per liter)

Solution A

Crystal violet	2.0g
Ethyl alcohol (95%)	20 ml

Solution B

Ammonium oxalate	0.8g
Distilled water	80.0 ml

Mix solution A and B. Store 24 h before use. Filter through a muslin cloth. Keep it in the storage bottle.

2. Gram's modification of Lugol 'solution (Per liter)

Iodine	1.0 g
Potassium iodide	2.0 g
Distilled water	300.0 ml

Allow iodine solution to dissolve several h or overnight in a room.

3. Decolorizers

i. Ethyl alcohol, 95%, slowest agent (mostly used).

ii. Acetone: fastest agent.

iii. Acetone- alcohol: intermediate (95% ethyl alcohol, 100 mL: 100mL).

With practice, any of the three decolorizing agents will yield good results.

4. Counter stain

Stock solution (per liter)

Saffranin	2.5 g
Ethyl alcohol, 95%	100.0 mL

Working solution (per liter)

Stock solution	10.0 mL
Distilled water	90.0 mL

Methods:

- On a clean slide, spread bacterial film and let it dry in air without heat.
- The smear was stained with crystal violet solution and kept it for 1 minute.
- The crystal violet solution was washed using tap water. Excess water was drained off and blot it dry with a paper towel.
- Then the smear was spate with iodine solution for a minute.
- Iodine solution was washed in tap water for a few seconds; blot it dry.
- Decolorized with solvent, e.g. Ethyl alcohol, until the solvent flows become colorless from the slide (~ 30 seconds) blot dries. The smear was rinsed with tap water for ~ 2 seconds.
- Counterstain for ~ 10 seconds with safranin solution was done.
- Then counterstain was washed curtly in tap water. The slide was dry with the help of blot paper and go for microscopic observation at 100X using immersion oil.
- Gram-positive bacteria blot purple to blue-black; gram-negative bacteria stain red.

2.4 Biochemical test (Denny and Hayward 2001)

2.4.1. Starch hydrolysis: The purpose is to see if the microbe can use starch, a complex carbohydrate made from glucose, as a source of carbon and energy for growth. Use of starch is accomplished by an enzyme called alpha-amylase

Medium composition:

Ingredients	Amount
Peptone	10.0 g
Beef extract	5.0 g
Starch (soluble)	2.0 g

Agar	20.0 g
Water	1000 mL
pH	7.0

The starch media was moist heat sterilized by autoclaving, then cooled at 45°Cand poured in Petri dishes for solidifying. For one rhizobacteria culture, 4 plates were maintained. The medium was spot inoculated by a 24 hr sold test rhizobacteria and incubate the plates at 28C for 72 h. To test starch hydrolysis one plate at a time after 72 h was taken. Flood the agar surface with Lugol's iodine; allow it acting for a few minutes. If starch is hydrolyzed, a tintless or reddish-brown zone was observed around the rhizobacterial colony growth in contrast to the blue background of the medium.

2.4.2. Catalase test: Smear a loopful of 24 h slant growth of the test bacterium was put on a glass slide and covered it with few drops of hydrogen peroxide. The reaction is + ve if the gas bubbles are produced.

2.4.3. Oxidase Test:

The oxidase is enzymes catalyzing the transfer of hydrogen directly to molecular oxygen resulting in the formation of water molecule. For oxidase test, a 24 h slant growth of the test rhizobacteria was streak on a filter paper saturated with 1% tetramethyl para phenylene-diaminodihydrogen chloride. The reaction is positive if a red or purple color appears within 10 seconds. The reaction is delayed positive if the color appears in 10-60 seconds.

2.4.4. Indoledisces Test:

With a plastic loop or glass loop spread suspected colony from Hi chrome UTI agar, modified (M1418) plate on DMACA indole discs. Observe for the appearance of red-pink color within 10-30 sec.

2.5 Antagonistic properties of PGPR strains against phytobacteria in vitro

Dual culture method was used for the screening of antagonistic properties of rhizobacteria such as *Bacillus amyloliquefaciens*, *B.cereus*, *B. pumilus* and *B. subtilis* against *Ralstoniasolanacearum*. The rhizobacteria were grown in nutrient broth medium for 24 h at 28 ±1C and maintained the population of phytobacteria (0.1 OD at 600nm). 100µlculture of *Ralstonia* sp. cultures were spread onto the Petri plates containing casein peptone glucose agar (CPG) medium to make a lawn of phytobacteria. Then three wells of 0.5 cm diameter were made in each Petri plate with a sterilized cork borer and 50 µLof 24 h old culture of PGPR strains like *Bacillus* sp. grown in the nutrient broth containing 0.1 OD at 600nm were poured into each well separately. The plates were incubated at 28 ±1C for 48 h and inhibition zone formed by PGPR strains was recorded. Those isolates, which did not form >0.5 cm diameter of inhibition zone, were not included in the study. The value of inhibition zone was converted into an area of inhibition zone using the formula: Area of circle = πr^2.

2.6 DNA extraction and screening of PGPRs (eg. Bacillus spp.)by PCR

The bacterial colonies were grown in Nutrient broth and incubated at 28±1°C with 200 rpm for 48 h. The bacterial cells were harvested in the form of pellet in the tubes by centrifugation for 8 min at 16,000 RCF (relative centrifugal force) in centrifuge and the supernatant was discarded. Total bacterial DNA was extracted by CTAB methods as described by Murray and Thompson (1980). For validation of primer, isolates of bacillus sp. was performed in a gradient thermal cycler (BIO-RAD C100TM Thermal cycler). The amplifications were carried out in a final volume of 25 µl of PCR master mix containing 5 µlof PCR buffer, 0.5µl of dNTPs (Promega), 0.5 µlof each primer, 1.5 µlMgCl$_2$, 0.25 µlof Taq polymerase and 100 ng of DNA template. In each PCR experiment, a control without a DNA template was used as a negative control. The denaturation of PCR 95C for 5 minute followed by ~30 second, annealing temperature was 54°C for 45 seconds for Difficidin, 58°C for 45 seconds for Bacillaene, and 50°C for 45 second for Macrolactin, extension were 1 min followed by 5 minute of final extension total 30 cycle were used in each PCR condition. A 25 µlaliquot of each amplified PCR product were separated on a 1.2% agarose gel 0.5% TAE buffer and stained with ethidium bromide. Gel electrophoresis unit was run on 60 V for 1.0 h and visualized under gel documentation (BIORAD, GEL DOC™ XR+ with imageLabTM software.

2.7 Method: Genomic DNA extraction by CTAB method

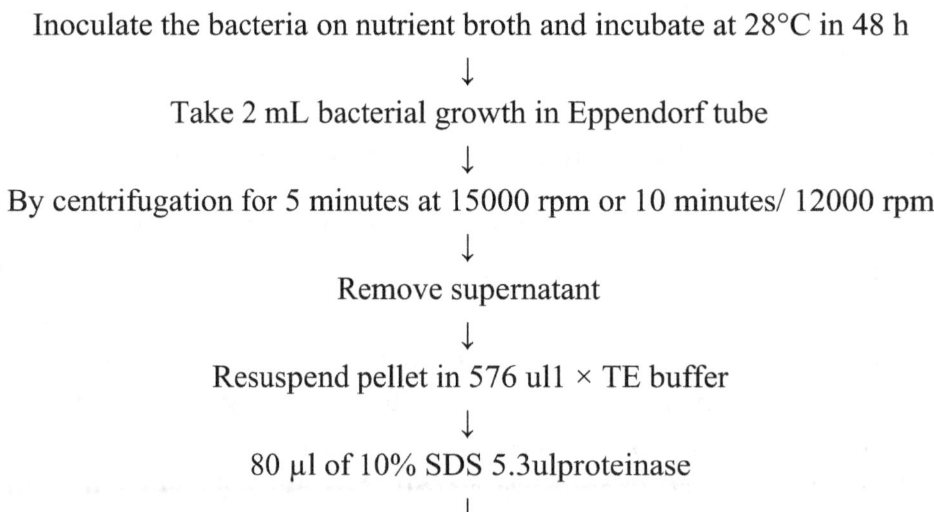

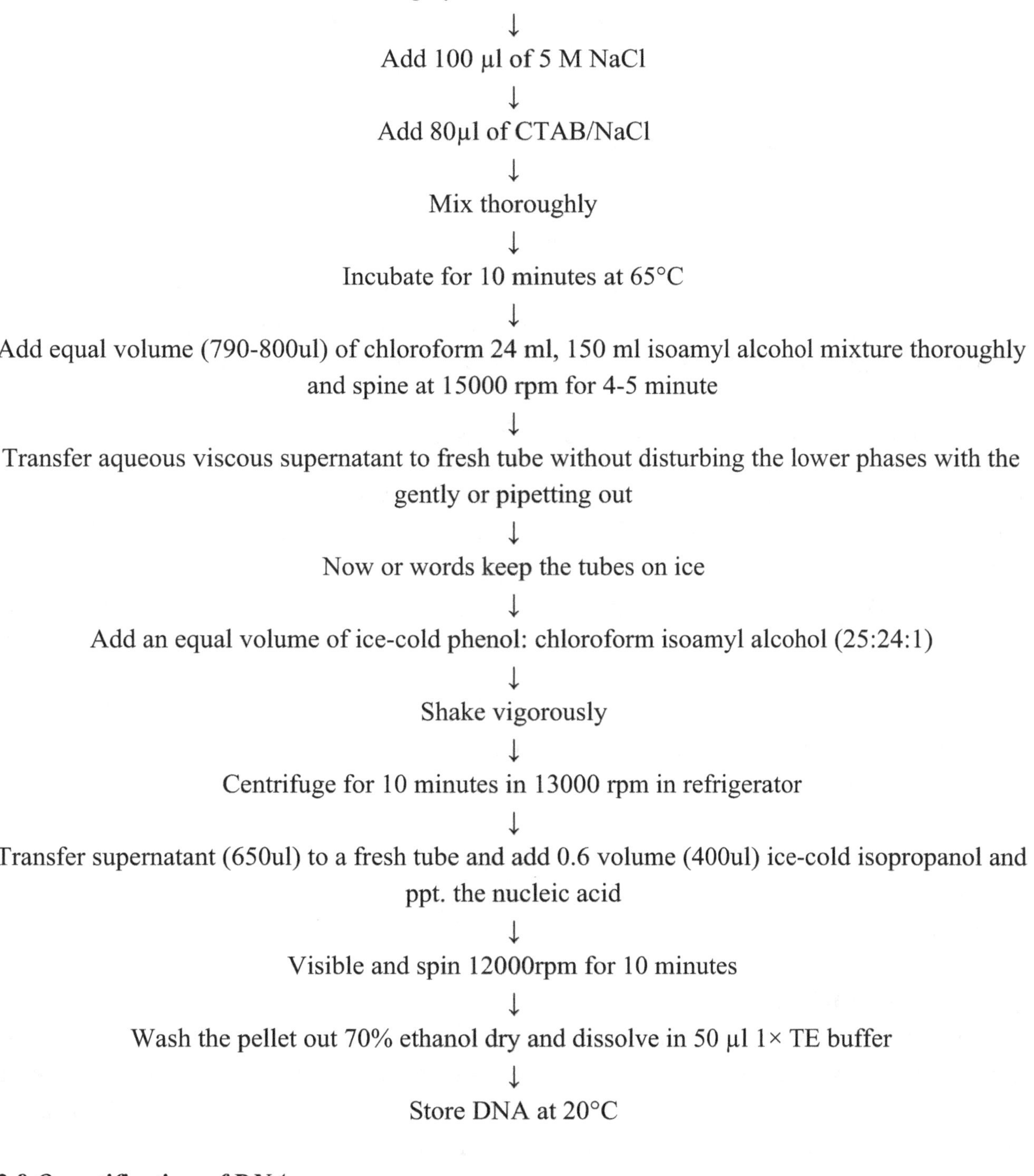

2.8 Quantification of DNA

By Gel electrophoresis method

Cast the agarose gel (0.8 %) in 50 x TAE buffer add ethidium bromide just before pouring. After solidification load the 5 µl of DNA samples with dye, and run the gel at 70 V for 2 h. View the gel under UV and take photographs.

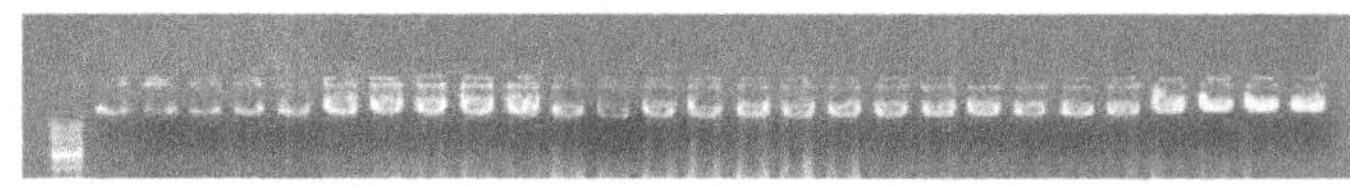

Fig. 8: Genomic DNA of rhizospheric bacteria isolated from chili

2.9 Quantification of bacterial DNA by Nanodrop:

After the isolation of genomic DNA, it was quantified by Nanodrop/ spectrophotometer. 1ul of DNA was used to analyze in nanodrop and the quantity of DNA (ng/µl) was recorded. For knowing the purity of DNA sample, the OD values were recorded at 260 and 280 nm.

2.10 Evaluation Plant Growth Promoting Rhizobacteria

The PGPR are known to influence the growth and improved the yield of crop plants besides enhancing soil health. These include direct effects such as auxin, or BNF such as production of metabolites against pathogenic bacteria.The rhizosphere soil samples of chili plants were isolated on nutrient agar medium and they were purified by streaking on the same medium. Purified cultures were maintained as purer culture with periodic transfer of fresh media and stocked for further use.

The Following attributes were studied for screening the bacterial isolates.
 (i) Ammonia Production
 (ii) Phosphate solubilization
(iii) Indole acetic acid (IAA) Production
(iv) HCN test
 (v) Siderophore production

i.) Ammonia Production
The different isolates of rhizobacteria were inoculated containing the peptone water. The tubes were incubated in incubation at 30°C for 4 days. 1ml of Nessler's reagent was added into each tube. The presence of a faint yellow color indicates a small amount of ammonia and deep yellow to brownish color indicates maximum production of ammonia.

ii)   Estimation of P-solubilization
For the rapid quantitative estimation of phosphate solubilization by the rhizobacteria pikovskaya medium was used, 24 h old cultures of all isolates of rhizobacteria were inoculated into the pikovskaya (PVK) medium and incubated at 28°C for 3 - 4 days. The isolates were spot

inoculated on PVK medium. Formation of transparent halo zone around the developing colonies indicatesP-solubilizing ability.

(iii) Production of indole acetic acid (IAA)

In this rhizobacterial isolates were inoculated in nutrient agar amended with L- Tryptophan and incubated at $37\,^{\circ}$C for 48 hrs. fully grown culture was centrifuged at 3000rpm for 30 min., the supernatant was mixed with two drops of ortho-phosphoric acid and 4 ml of the salkowski reagent (50 ml 35% of perchloric acid, 1ml of 0.5M $FeCl_3$ solution. Development of pink color was indicative of IAA production.

(iv) Hydrogen cyanide (HCN) test

Production of HCN was determined using the modified procedure of Millar and Higgins. All the bacterial strains were grown on trypticase soy agar (TSA) plates. Sterilized Whatman no.1 filter paper strips were soaked in picric acid solution (2.5 g of picric acid, 12.5g of Na_2CO_3, in 1000 mL of distilled water) and were placed in the lid of each petri dish. Dishes were sealed with parafilm and incubated at $28 \pm 1\,^{\circ}$Cfor 48 h. A change in color of the filter paper strip from tallow to light brown, brown and reddish-brown was recorded as an indication of weak, moderate or strong production of HCN by each strain, respectively.

(v) Screening for siderophore production

The tertiary complex, Chromeazural- S (CAS) serves as an indicator; 48 hrs.old cultures of the strains were streaked onto the nutrition agar medium amended with indicator dye. The development of a bright zone with yellowish fluorescent color by the culture in the dark color medium indicated siderophore production.Based on the color the result was scored either negative or positive to this test, change of the medium from blue to fluorescent yellow while no color change indicated the absence of siderophore production.

(a)

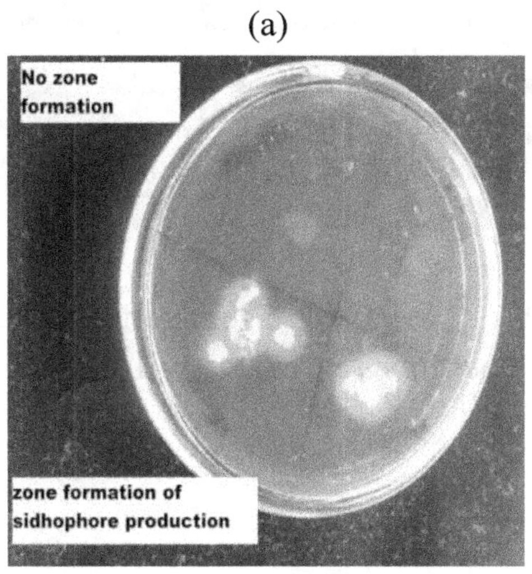

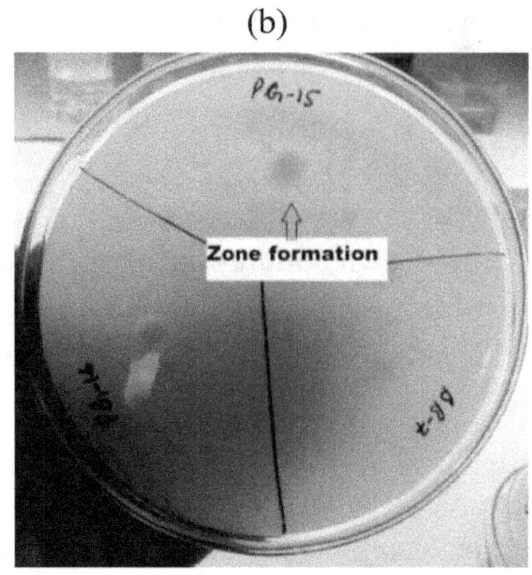

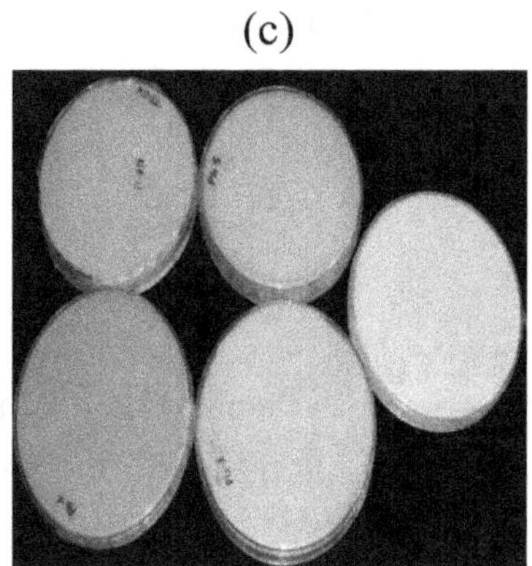

Fig. 9: Plant growth-promoting ability of rhizobacteria. **(a)** Siderophoresproduction **(b)** Phosphorous production **(c)** HCN test **(d)**Ammonia production

3. Conclusions

The human population continues to grow in the geometric way as compares to arithmetic growth of food production that means we required to produce more food. Fifty years ago, the Green Revolution increased agricultural production worldwide, saving millions of people from starvation and undernourishment. But the advancement in chemicals fertilizers, pesticides lead to the destruction of soil health as well as soil microflora. Thus an alternative approach in the form of plant growth-promoting rhizobacteria (PGPR) is required for the sustainable development of agriculture. The PGPRs also is known as plant growth-promoting microorganisms, play a significant role in the intensively managed agricultural systems. The rising demand for crop production with a significant reduction in synthetic chemical fertilizers and pesticides use is a challenge. The use of PGPR has been proven to be an environment-friendly way of increasing crop productivity by facilitating plant growth through either a direct or indirect mechanism. The mechanisms of PGPR include curbing hormonal and nutritional harmony, inducing systemic resistance against phytopathogens, and solubilizing nutrients for easy uptake by crops. The plant growth-promoting bacteria having the ability of the isolate to produce IAA, as IAA directly influences root growth, development and enhancing nutrient uptake. The phosphorous influences overall plant growth and root development. The PGPR utilization as biofertilizers will determine a sustainable promotion of host plant growth. PGPR act as model systems which provide a pathway to constitute novel genetic library and bioactive chemicals which diversely uses in agriculture and environmental sustainability

PGPR also show synergistic and antagonistic interactions with pathogens within the rhizosphere. There are several bacterial species that act as PGPR, described in the literature like Bacillus, Pseudomonas, arthrobacter, etc as successful in improving plant growth. However, there is a gap between the mode of action of the PGPR for plant growth and the role of the PGPR as biofertilizer. The advancement in OMICS techniques like genomics, transcriptomics, proteomics, metabolomics reveals the secret of host-pathogen interaction and mode of action of rhizobacteria in plant growth. The focus of further Future research will be on optimizing growth condition and enhanced shelf life of PGPR products, non-phytotoxic, tolerance to adverse environmental conditions, higher yield and cost-effective PGPR products, to uplift the economic and social status and livelihood of our farmers

References

1. Bakker PAHM,Berendsen RL, Doornbos RF, Wintermans PCA, and Pieterse CMJ (2013) The rhizosphere revisited: root microbiomics. Frontier in plant science 4:165.

2. Berendsen RL, Pieterse CM, Bakker PAHM (2012) Therhizospheremicrobiome and plant health. Trends in Plant Science 17: 478-486.

3. Bereswill SP, Bugert I Bruchmuller, Gider K (1995). Identification of the fire blight

4. pathogen, Erwiniaamylovora, by PCR assays with chromosomal DNA. Appl. Environ.Microbiol 61(7): 2636-2642.

5. Bestel-Corre G, Dumas-Gaudot E, Poinsot V, Dieu M, Dierick JF, van Tuinen D, RemacleJ,Gianinazzi-Pearson V, Gianinazzi S (2002) Proteome analysis and identification of symbiosis related proteins from MedicagotruncatulaGaertn. by two-dimensional electrophoresis and mass spectrometry. Electrophoresis 23:122–137.

6. Bevivino A, Sarrocco S, Dalmastri C, TabacchioniS,Cantale C, Chiarini L (1998) Characterization of a free living maize rhizosphere population of *Burkholderiacepacia*: effect of seed treatment on disease suppression and growth promotion of maize. FEMS.Microbiol. Ecol. 27(3): 225-237

7. Birch PR, Hyman LJ, Taylor R, Opio AF, Bragard C, Toth IK (1997) RAPD PCR based differentiation of *Xanthomonascampestris*pv. *phaseoli* and *Xanthomonascampestris*pv. *phaseoli* var. *fuscans*. Eur. J. Plant. Pathol 103(9): 809-814.

8. Braud A, Jézéquel K, Bazot S, Lebeau T (2009) Enhanced phytoextraction of an agricultural Cr- and Pb-contaminated soil by bioaugmentation with siderophore-producing bacteria. Chemosphere 74:280–286.

9. Camacho C, Coulouris G, Avagyan V, Ma N, Papadopoulos J, et al. (2009) BLAST+: architecture and applications. BMC Bioinformatics 10: 421.

10. Choudhary DK, Sharma KP, Gaur RK (2011) Biotechnological perspectives of microbes in agro-ecosystems. Biotechnol.Lett, 33: 1905–1910.

11. Darling ACE, Mau B, Blattner FR, Perna NT (2004) Mauve: multiple alignment of conserved genomic sequence with rearrangements. Genome Res 14: 1394–403.

12. Denny, T. P., & Hayward, A. C. (2001). Gram-negative bacteria: Ralstonia. In N. W. Schaad, J. B. Jones, & W. Chun (Eds.), Laboratory guide for identification of plant pathogenic bacteria (pp. 151-174, 3rd edn). APS Press, St. Paul, M. N

13. Deslippe JR, Egger KN (2006) Molecular diversity of nifH genes from bacteria associated with high arctic dwarf shrubs. Microbial Ecology 51:516–525.

14. Dumas-Gaudot E (2004) Proteomics as a way to identify extra-radicular fungal proteins from Glomusintraradices— RiT-DNA carrot root mycorrhizas.Fems Microbiology Ecology 48: 401-411.

15. Gajbhiye A, Bhandarkar M, Dongre A, Meshram S (2007). Genetic Diversity Evaluation of Bacillus isolates using Randomly Amplified Polymorphic DNA molecular marker. Rom. Biotech.Lett. 12(3): 3277

16. Glick BR (1995) The enhancement of plant growth by free living bacteria. Can J Microbiol 41:109-14.

17. Gosal AE , Saroa B , Vikal C , Cameotra D, Pathania A, Bhanot A (2011) Isolation and molecular characterisation of diazotrophic growth-promoting bacteria from wheat rhizospheric soils of Punjab. Soil Research 49:725–732.

18. Gupta A, Gopal M, Thomas GV, Manikandan V, Gajewski J, Thomas G, Seshagiri S, Schuster SC, Rajesh P, Gupta R (2014) Whole Genome Sequencing and Analysis of Plant Growth Promoting Bacteria Isolated from the Rhizosphere of Plantation Crops Coconut, Cocoa and Arecanut. PLosOne 9(8): 14

19. Hurek T, Reinhold-Hurek B (2003) Azoarcus sp. Strain BH72 as a model for nitrogen-fixing grass endophytes. J Biotechnol 106:169-78.

20. Jones P, Binns D, Chang HY, Fraser M, Li W (2014) InterProScan 5: genome-scale protein function classification. Bioinformatics.

21. Joseph B, Patra RR, Lawrence R (2007) Characterization of plant growth promoting rhizobacteria associated   with chickpea (*Cicerrietinum* L). Int J Plant Prod 1:141-52.

22. Kasa P, Modugapalem H, Battini K (2015) Isolation, screening, and molecular characterization of plant growth promoting rhizobacteria isolates of Azotobacter and Trichoderma and their beneficial activities. Journal of Natural Science, Biology and Medicine 6(2):360-363.

23. Kelley DR, Liu B, Delcher AL, Pop M, Salzberg SL (2012) Gene prediction with Glimmer for metagenomic sequences augmented by classification and clustering. Nucleic Acids 40(1):9.

24. Khan AG (2005) Role of soil microbes in the rhizospheres of plants growing on trace metal contaminated soils in phytoremediation. J Trace Elem Med Biol 18:355-64

25. Kloepper JW, Lifshitz R, Schroth MN (1988) Pseudomonas inoculants to benefit plant production. AnimPlant   Sci. 1: 60-4.

26. Konstantinidis KT, Tiedje JM (2004) Trends between gene content and genome size in prokaryotic species with larger genomes. ProcNatlAcadSci U S A 101: 3160–3165

27. Kumar A, Maurya B R, and Raghuwanshi R (2014) Isolation and characterization of PGPR and their effect on growth, yield and nutrient content in wheat (*Triticumaestivum* L.)Biocatal. Agric. Biotechnol. 3: 121–128.

28. Larkin M A, G Blackshields, N Brown, R. Chenna P A, McGettigan H, McWilliam F, Valentin I M, Wallace A Wilm, R. Lopez (2007). Clustal W and Clustal X version 2.0. Bioinformatics 23(21): 2947-2948.

29. Liao VH Ch, Chien MT, Tseng YY, Ou KL (2006) Assessment of heavy metal bioavailability in contaminated sediments and soils using green fluorescent protein-based bacterial biosensors. Environ Pollut 142:17–23

30. Magrane M, Consortium U (2011) UniProt Knowledgebase: a hub of integrated protein data. Database (Oxford) 2011: bar009.

31. Mahbouba B, Christine LR, Nadir B, Nadia Y, Abdelhamid D (2013) Phenotypic and molecular characterization of plant growth promoting Rhizobacteria isolated from the rhizosphere of wheat (*TriticumdurumDesf.*) in Algeria. African Journal of Microbiology Research. 7(23): 2893-2904

32. Majeed A, Abbasi MK, Hameed S, Imran A and Rahim N (2015) Isolation and characterization of plant growth promoting rhizobacteria from wheat rhizosphere and their growth effects on plant growth promotion. Frontiers in microbiology. 6:198

33. Matilla MA, Pizarro-Tobias P, Roca A, Fernandez M, Duque E (2011) Complete genome of the plant growth-promoting rhizobacterium*Pseudomonas putida* BIRD-1. J Bacteriol 193: 1290

34. Morris AC, Djordjevic MA (2006) The Rhizobium *Leguminosarumbiovartrifolii* ANU794 induces novel developmental responses on the subterranean clover cultivar Woogenellup. Mol Plant Microbe Interact 19:471–479

35. Narula N, Kumar V, Singh B, Bhatia R, and Laxminarayana K (2005).Impact of biofertilizers on grain yield in spring wheat under varying fertility conditions and wheat-cotton rotation. Arch. Agron. Soil Sci. 51:79–89.

36. Paffetti D, Scotti C, Gnocchi S, Fancelli S, Bazzicalupo M (1996) Genetic diversity of an Italian Rhizobium meliloti population from different *Medicagosativa* varieties. Appl. Environ. Microbiol 62(7): 2279-2285

37. Park M, Kim C, Yang J, Lee H, Shin W, Kim S, Sa T (2005) Isolation and characterization of diazotrophic growth promoting bacteria from rhizosphere of agricultural crops of Korea. Microbiological Research 160:127–133.

38. Peck SC, Nuhse TS, Hess D, Iglesias A, Meins F, Boller T (2001) Directed proteomics identifies a plant-specific protein rapidly phosphorylated in response to bacterial and fungal elicitors. Plant Cell 13:1467–1475

39. Saharan BS, Nehra V (2011). Plant growth promoting rhizobacteria: a critical review. Life Sci. Med. Res 21: 1-30

40. Saitou, Nei (1987) The neighbour-joining method: a new method for reconstructing phylogenetic tress. Molecular biology and evolutional. 4:406-425

41. Sakthivel NS, Gnanamanickam S. (1987). Evaluation of Pseudomonas fluorescence for suppression of sheath rot disease and for enhancement of grain yields in rice (*Oryzasativa* L.). Applied and Environmental Microbiology., 53, 2056-2059.

42. Schenk PM, Kazan K, Wilson I, Anderson JP, Richmond T, Somerville SC, Manners JM (2000) Coordinated plant defense responses in Arabidopsis revealed by microarray analysis. Proc. Natl. Acad. Sci. U.S.A. 97:11655–11660.

43. Schulze A, Downward J (2001). Navigating gene expression microarrays - a technology review. Nature Cell Biology 3: E190-E195.

44. Shaharoona B, Naveed M, Arshad M, Zahir Z A (2008).Fertilizer dependent efficiency of Pseudomonads for improving growth, yield, andnutrient use efficiency of wheat (*Triticumaestivum* L.). Appl. Microbiol. Biotechnol. 79: 147–155.

45. Shaheen T, Khan AA, Mahmood- ur-Rahman, Qamar MTU, Rahman M (2015) Estimation of genetic diversity of plant growth promoting rhizobacteria (PGPR) strains found in different areas of Pakistan using rapd and 16s rRNA analysis. The Journal of Animal & Plant Sciences, 25(5):1457-1465.

46. Srivastava S, Chaudhry V, Mishra A, Chauhan PS, Rehman A, Yadav A, Tuteja A, NautiyalCS (2012) Gene expression profiling through microarray analysis in *Arabidopsis thaliana* colonized by *Pseudomonas putida* MTCC5279, a plant growth promoting rhizobacterium. Plant Signalling & Behaviour. 2: 235-245

47. Whipps JM, McQquilken MP, BudgeSS (1993) Use of fungal antagonists for biocontrolof damping-off and *Sclerotinia*disease. Pestic Sci 37:309-13.

48. Williams JGK, Kubelik AR, Livak KJ, Rafalski JA, Tingey SV (1990) DNA polymorphisms amplified by arbitrary primers are useful as genetic markers. Nucleic Acids Res, 18, 6531-6535.

49. Yasmin T, Tabbasam N, Ullah I, Asif M, Zafar Y (2008) Studying the extent of genetic diversity among *Gossypiumarboreum* L. genotypes/cultivars using DNA fingerprinting. Genet.Resour. Crop.Ev. 55(3): 331-339.